QUANTUM BUSINESS

ARCHITECT YOUR LEGACY:
LEAD WITH SOUL AND
MAKE CONSCIOUS DECISIONS
THAT MATTER

Jivi Saran, MBA, DBA(c)

Quantum Business
Copyright © 2025 by Jivi Saran, MBA, DBA(c)

All rights reserved. No part of this publication may be reproduced, distributed, or transmitted in any form or by any means, including photocopying, recording, or other electronic or mechanical methods, without the prior written permission of the author, except in the case of brief quotations embodied in critical reviews and certain other non-commercial uses permitted by copyright law.

Tellwell Talent
www.tellwell.ca

ISBN
978-1-8341-8296-4 (Hardcover)
978-1-8341-8297-1 (Paperback)

Dedication

This book is dedicated to the courageous entrepreneurs, innovative leaders, and compassionate change-makers who dare to dream beyond the limitations of traditional business models. To those who understand that true success lies not only in accumulating wealth but in cultivating a world where profit and purpose are inextricably intertwined. To those who choose to lead with consciousness, embracing the interconnectedness of all things and striving to create a more just and sustainable future for generations to come. This is for those who embody the spirit of the Quantum Business paradigm – a testament to your unwavering commitment to a higher calling, a testament to your belief in the power of human potential to transform the world of business and beyond. It is a testament to your unwavering belief that a more equitable and sustainable future is not just a possibility, but a responsibility we all share. To each of you, thank you for inspiring us all to strive for a better tomorrow. Your dedication to conscious business practices reminds us that true success is measured not solely by financial metrics but by the positive impact we leave on the world. This work is dedicated to your vision and tireless efforts.

Preface

The journey to writing this book began not in a boardroom, but in a quiet space of reflection. It emerged from a deep-seated belief that the traditional models of business are no longer sufficient for navigating the complex challenges of our time. The world demands a new approach—a paradigm shift that acknowledges the interconnectedness of our actions and the far-reaching consequences of our decisions. This is not just about tweaking existing strategies; it's about fundamentally reimagining the role of business in society.

My own experiences as an executive coach and consultant have brought me face-to-face with the limitations of conventional leadership styles and the urgent need for a more holistic and conscious approach. I've witnessed firsthand the transformative power of integrating spiritual principles into business practices, fostering cultures of compassion, collaboration, and purpose-driven innovation.

Through countless conversations and collaborations with visionary leaders, I have gained invaluable insights into the challenges and opportunities presented by the transition to a quantum business model. This book encapsulates these learnings and insights, offering a practical framework and actionable strategies for creating businesses that are not only profitable but also profoundly beneficial to all stakeholders. It's a call to action for those seeking a more meaningful and impactful business journey, a journey that aligns the pursuit of profit with the pursuit of a better world. The path ahead is not without its obstacles, but the potential rewards – a future where both profit and purpose thrive in harmony – are immensely worthwhile.

Introduction

The world of business is at a crossroads. Traditional capitalist models, rooted in a linear and mechanistic worldview, are struggling to address the complexities of a rapidly changing global landscape. Climate change, social inequality, and technological disruption are forcing us to reconsider the very foundations of how we do business. This book argues that a radical shift is necessary—a quantum leap from outdated methodologies to a more conscious and holistic approach. We need a new paradigm, a new way of thinking about business that moves beyond profit maximization as the sole metric of success.

Quantum Business proposes such a paradigm. It's a framework that draws upon the insights of quantum physics to illuminate the interconnectedness of all things, emphasizing the profound impact our decisions have on the broader ecosystem. It's about recognizing that a business is not an isolated entity, but an integral part of a complex web of relationships that extends far beyond its immediate stakeholders. Unlike classical physics, which views the universe as a collection of separate, predictable components, quantum physics reveals a world characterized by uncertainty, interconnectedness, and the profound influence of observation. These principles, translated into the business world, offer a powerful lens through which to examine leadership, strategy, and organizational culture. This book will explore the key principles of Quantum Business, providing practical strategies and real-world examples of how organizations can integrate these principles into their operations. We'll delve into the importance of conscious leadership, the cultivation of spiritual intelligence, and the pursuit of eudaimonia (human flourishing) as critical components of building sustainable and truly successful businesses. It's a journey of transformation, inviting you to question your assumptions, expand your perspectives, and ultimately, create a more meaningful and impactful business legacy. Are you ready to embark on this quantum leap?

Table of Contents

Dedication iii
Preface v
Introduction vii
Chapter 1: The Evolution of Business and Leadership 1
    1. The Evolution of Business Thinking 3
    2. The Limitations of Traditional Capitalism 8
    3. The Status-Quo Leadership- Barrier to Long-Term Success 13
    4. The Urgency for Change 17
    5. The New Business Landscape: Adaptability and Interconnectedness.. 20
Chapter 2: The Quantum Business Paradigm.......................... 23
    1. Introducing the Quantum Business Paradigm................ 25
    2. The Imperative for Quantum Leadership 30
Chapter 3: Conscious Decision-Making and Leadership 35
    1. The Role of Conscious Leadership 37
    2. Conscious Decision-Making: The Art of Intentional Choices...42
    3. Leading with Empathy and Emotional Intelligence 46
    4. Benefits of Conscious Decision-Making........................ 50
    5. Challenges in Conscious Decision-Making.................... 52
    6. How to Develop Conscious Decision-Making Skills 54

    7. Moving from Linear Decision-Making to Quantum Business Thinking 57

Chapter 4: Critical Thinking and Ethical Leadership 61
    1. Critical Thinking: The Foundation of Effective Decision-Making.. 63
    2. Understanding Critical Thinking...................................... 65
    3. The Importance of Critical Thinking................................ 68
    4. Challenges in Developing Critical Thinking 71
    5. How to Improve Critical Thinking Skills 74

Chapter 5: The Intersection of Business, Spirituality, and Purpose....77
    1. Integrating Spirituality and Business 79
    2. Developing Your Spiritual Intelligence 85
    3. Holistic Decision Making and Systems Thinking 92
    4. Harnessing Intuition in Decision Making........................ 98
    5. Cultivating Mindfulness and Presence 103
    6. Ethical Frameworks for Decision Making..................... 109
    7. The Power of Forgiveness and Letting Go.................... 115

Chapter 6: Conscious Capitalism in Action 121
    1. Measuring Impact Beyond the Bottom Line 123
    2. Defining Your Company's Higher Purpose 128
    3. Creating a Values Based Culture.................................. 133
    4. Empowering Employees Through Purpose................... 138
    5. Building Ethical Supply Chains and Partnerships.......... 143
    6. Transparency and Accountability in Operations 148

Chapter 7: Business as a Force for Good 153
    1. The Pursuit of Eudaimonia Human Flourishing in the Workplace.. 155
    2. Embracing Interconnectedness in Supply Chains 160
    3. The Role of Business in Social and Environmental Change.. 165
    4. Building a Sustainable and Regenerative Economy....... 171

 5. Inspiring the Next Generation of Conscious Leaders 176
 6. Cultivating a Culture of Purpose and Meaning 181

Chapter 8: Case Studies in Conscious Business 187
 1. Patagonia A Model of Conscious Capitalism 189
 2. Unilever's Sustainable Living Plan 194
 3. Seventh Generation Environmental Sustainability in Action 199
 4. Eight Case Studies of Conscious Businesses from Various Sectors 205

Chapter 9: The Future of Quantum Business 211
 1. The Future of Conscious Capitalism 213
 2. A Call to Action Embracing the Quantum Leap 219
 3. Challenges and Future Prospects 225

Chapter 10: Quantum Business for C-Suite Leaders 231
 1. Quantum Architect: Designing the Future Through Quantum Principles 233
 2. Quantum Innovation: Redefining Creativity in a Quantum World 239
 3. Quantum Personal Excellence: A New Paradigm in Human Potential 245
 4. Quantum Emotional Intelligence for C-Suite Leaders ... 251
 5. Quantum Communication Clarity for C-Suite Leaders 256
 6. The Quantum Intuition Engine for C-Suite Leaders 261
 7. Quantum Energy Management and Resilience for C-Suite Leaders 267
 8. Quantum Conscious Capitalism and Sustainability for C-Suite Leaders 272
 9. The Quantum Approach to Sustainable Business Practices 276
 10. Quantum Strategic Foresight and Scenario Planning for C-Suite Leaders 279
 11. Quantum Wealth and Value Creation for C-Suite Leaders 285

Conclusion 291
    1. The Quantum Imperative for Leadership 293
Acknowledgments 299
Glossary 301
References 303
Author Biography 305

Chapter 1: The Evolution of Business and Leadership

1. The Evolution of Business Thinking

The traditional models of business thinking have been built on Newtonian principles—linear cause-and-effect logic, hierarchical decision-making, and rigid structures. While these methods worked in stable and predictable markets, they no longer serve organizations in an era defined by uncertainty, rapid technological advancements, and global interconnectedness.

The rise of Quantum Business requires a paradigm shift, one that moves beyond outdated economic principles and embraces a multidimensional, systems-thinking approach. This shift is essential for businesses to not only survive but thrive in a rapidly evolving landscape where traditional decision-making models are insufficient.

This chapter will explore how business thinking has evolved, the limitations of past decision-making approaches, and why Quantum Business and conscious capitalism are the future of organizational success.

The Industrial Era and the Birth of Linear Business Models

During the Industrial Revolution, businesses operated under a command-and-control structure, heavily influenced by mechanistic thinking. These organizations valued:

- Predictability and control: Efficiency and mass production were prioritized over adaptability.

- Centralized decision-making: Power was concentrated at the top, with little input from employees.
- Short-term profit focus: The primary goal was immediate financial return, with minimal consideration for long-term sustainability.

While these principles helped businesses scale during the 19th and early 20th centuries, they also led to significant challenges, including worker exploitation, environmental degradation, and economic inequalities.

Why Past Decision-Making Models Will No Longer Work

Traditional business strategies focused on predictability and risk reduction, but today's world demands fluidity and responsiveness. The limitations of old models include:

- Linear Forecasting Fails in Uncertain Environments: Static five-year strategic plans quickly become obsolete in industries facing constant disruption.
- Top-Down Decision Making Stifles Innovation: In rapidly changing industries, innovation must come from all levels of an organization, not just the executive suite.
- Profit-First Mentalities Undermine Sustainability: Businesses that prioritize short-term shareholder returns over long-term stakeholder well-being lose competitive advantages.

The Shift Toward Systems Thinking and Conscious Capitalism

As markets matured, businesses began recognizing that rigid hierarchies and short-term financial strategies were not sustainable. The late 20th century saw the rise of:

- Stakeholder capitalism, where companies began considering employees, customers, communities, and shareholders in decision-making.

- Corporate social responsibility (CSR) as a strategy to align business practices with ethical considerations.
- The digital economy, which introduced new challenges and opportunities that required agile and decentralized structures.

Despite these advancements, many organizations still operate under linear models of strategy and planning, failing to account for complexity, uncertainty, and interconnectedness.

The Emergence of Quantum Business Thinking

Just as quantum mechanics revolutionized physics by revealing that matter and energy are interconnected and probabilistic, Quantum Business Thinking challenges the notion of rigid business structures. It emphasizes:

- Interconnectedness: Recognizing that businesses do not operate in isolation but within complex, dynamic ecosystems.
- Adaptability: Shifting from rigid strategies to agile, continuously evolving models.
- Holistic decision-making: Factoring in economic, social, and environmental considerations to create long-term value.

Quantum Business requires leaders to embrace uncertainty rather than fear it, leveraging it as an opportunity for innovation and growth.

Quantum Business as the Future of Leadership

To navigate the future successfully, leaders must develop new competencies that align with the Quantum Business Framework:

1. Superposition Thinking: Holding multiple possibilities at once rather than relying on a single, linear strategy.

2. Quantum Entanglement: Understanding the deep interconnectivity between markets, economies, and societal needs.
3. Quantum Tunneling: Finding innovative solutions to previously insurmountable barriers through unconventional strategies.
4. Observer Effect in Leadership: Recognizing that leadership presence and mindset shape the outcomes within an organization.

This chapter has laid the foundation for understanding why past business models must evolve and how Quantum Business Thinking will shape the next generation of leadership.

Reflection

2. The Limitations of Traditional Capitalism

The relentless pursuit of profit maximization, a cornerstone of traditional capitalism, has yielded undeniable economic growth. However, this success has come at a significant cost, frequently neglecting crucial aspects of long-term sustainability, social equity, and environmental responsibility. The inherent flaw lies in the system's prioritization of short-term gains over the well-being of people and the planet. This myopic focus fosters a culture where ethical considerations are often sacrificed at the altar of immediate financial returns, leading to a cascade of detrimental consequences.

One stark illustration is the 2008 global financial crisis, a direct result of unchecked risk-taking and a culture of short-term profit maximization within the financial sector. The pursuit of lucrative, yet ultimately unsustainable, investment strategies, coupled with a lack of regulatory oversight, triggered a domino effect that devastated global economies and left millions facing financial ruin. The crisis exposed the fragility of a system built on short-term gains and the devastating consequences of neglecting long-term systemic risks. It served as a stark reminder that economic stability requires a more balanced and holistic approach. Prior to the economic disruptions caused by the COVID-19 pandemic (Tooze, 2023), the *Financial Times* introduced a platform called *The New Agenda*, advocating for a fundamental "reset" of capitalism (Financial Times, 2019).

Beyond the realm of finance, countless examples highlight the environmental devastation wrought by prioritizing profit over planetary health. The unchecked exploitation of natural resources, driven by the insatiable demand for cheap goods and services, has led to deforestation, depletion of vital resources, and catastrophic levels of pollution. The consequences are evident in climate change, biodiversity loss, and the increasing frequency of extreme weather events. These are not merely abstract environmental concerns; they are tangible threats impacting human health, livelihoods, and global stability.

Corporate scandals further illuminate the ethical failings of traditional capitalism. Numerous instances of companies prioritizing profit over ethical considerations have resulted in widespread harm, from worker exploitation to dangerous product recalls and environmental damage. Cases like the Deepwater Horizon oil spill, where the pursuit of cost savings led to a catastrophic disaster with devastating environmental and social consequences, underscore the moral bankruptcy of systems prioritizing profit above all else. These incidents highlight the urgent need for a paradigm shift, one that prioritizes ethical considerations and long-term sustainability alongside financial success.

The limitations of traditional capitalism extend beyond environmental damage and corporate malfeasance. The widening gap between the rich and the poor, a defining characteristic of many capitalist economies, exposes a system that often exacerbates inequality rather than promoting social equity. The focus on shareholder value frequently leads to decisions that prioritize profit over employee well-being, resulting in low wages, precarious employment, and a lack of opportunities for social mobility.

This not only fuels social unrest but also undermines the overall health and productivity of the workforce. Furthermore, the emphasis on material consumption inherent in traditional capitalism fosters a culture of dissatisfaction and a relentless pursuit of more, often at the expense of genuine human connection and fulfillment. The constant bombardment of advertising and marketing campaigns promotes a cycle of acquisition that leaves many feeling unfulfilled and disconnected from themselves and their communities. This relentless focus on materialistic pursuits often overshadows the importance of personal growth, meaningful relationships, and a sense of purpose, ultimately hindering genuine human flourishing.

The very foundation of traditional capitalism rests on the assumption of infinite growth within a finite system—a paradoxical notion that is increasingly unsustainable. The planet's resources are finite, and the current rate of consumption is far exceeding the Earth's capacity to replenish them. Continuing down this path will inevitably lead to ecological collapse and a catastrophic disruption of the global economy. The World Bank projects that by 2050, 216 million people will be displaced as internal climate migrants (Clement et al., 2021), while the global economy is expected to lose $23 trillion (Flavelle, 2021). These staggering projections, combined with the failure to stay on track with the Paris Agreement's 1.5°C target, as revealed at COP 28 in 2023 (UNFCCC, 2023), highlight the urgent need for an economic paradigm shift. The consequences of climate change are no longer abstract or distant—they are unfolding in real time, reinforcing the necessity of transitioning towards a more sustainable and equitable system. If left unchecked, the current trajectory will accelerate what climate scientists have termed the "sixth mass extinction" (Barnosky et al., 2011). The time for incremental adjustments has passed; we must now engage in a radical reassessment of economic principles, prioritizing regenerative and conscious capitalism to ensure long-term planetary and economic stability.

This critique of traditional capitalism is not intended to dismiss the system entirely. Capitalism, when properly regulated and guided by ethical principles, can be a powerful engine for innovation and economic growth. However, the current model, with its unchecked focus on short-term profits and disregard for long-term consequences, is clearly unsustainable.

A transformation is required, a shift towards a more conscious and holistic approach to business that integrates ethical considerations, environmental sustainability, and social equity as core principles. This shift requires a fundamental rethinking of the relationship between business, society, and the environment. It calls for a new paradigm, one that recognizes the interconnectedness of all things and prioritizes the well-being of both people and the planet alongside the pursuit of economic success. This is the essence of the Quantum Business paradigm, which we will explore in the following sections. This new model embraces a holistic view, acknowledging the interconnectedness of all stakeholders and recognizing the far-reaching consequences of business decisions, thereby laying the foundation for a more sustainable and equitable future. By adopting the Quantum way, businesses can transcend the limitations of linear economic thinking and cultivate regenerative ecosystems that not only drive profitability but also restore balance to society and the environment, fostering resilience, innovation, and long-term prosperity.

Reflection

3. The Status-Quo Leadership- Barrier to Long-Term Success

Status quo leadership is a reactive, maintenance-driven approach that prioritizes stability, short-term results, and operational efficiency over long-term innovation and transformation. Leaders operating under this model focus on preserving existing structures and processes rather than adapting to or shaping the future. While maintaining stability can be beneficial in the short run, an over-reliance on this leadership style leads to stagnation and vulnerability, especially in industries experiencing rapid disruption.

One of the defining characteristics of status quo leadership is its short-term focus over long-term vision. Leaders in this mode often prioritize quarterly earnings, immediate performance metrics, and maintaining existing operations instead of investing in future sustainability. A striking example is Kodak, a company that invented the digital camera in 1975 but failed to embrace digital photography for fear of cannibalizing its profitable film business. This reluctance to adapt led to Kodak's eventual bankruptcy in 2012, as competitors successfully capitalized on the shift to digital.

Another major flaw of status quo leadership is its resistance to change and innovation. Organizations operating under this paradigm tend to make superficial adjustments rather than fundamental, forward-thinking changes. Leaders may recognize that their industries are evolving, yet they hesitate to embrace the necessary transformation, fearing disruption to their current business models. This reluctance results in organizations becoming reactive problem solvers rather than proactive innovators. Instead of anticipating market changes and acting decisively, they respond to disruptions only when forced, often when it is too late.

A further issue is micro-management and operational control, where leaders remain overly involved in routine operations, slowing down decision-making and innovation. This can lead to inefficient management practices, such as status update meetings that focus on tracking progress rather than enabling meaningful improvements. Additionally, leadership pipelines suffer in organizations stuck in the status quo, as leaders fail to prioritize succession planning and talent development. Many fear developing future leaders who could eventually replace them, creating a long-term leadership vacuum that weakens the organization's resilience and adaptability.

Perhaps the greatest risk of status quo leadership is the failure to recognize market shifts and emerging trends. Organizations stuck in outdated business models often ignore early warning signs of industry transformation. As seen in Kodak's case, such a failure can be fatal. In contrast, proactive organizations like Cirque du Soleil thrive by redefining industries instead of clinging to traditional models. Rather than competing in the declining circus industry, Cirque transformed live entertainment by eliminating animal acts, integrating artistic storytelling, and targeting premium audiences. This visionary approach allowed it to dominate a completely new entertainment niche.

Another classic case of **status quo leadership failure** is **Blockbuster**, which refused to acknowledge the changing landscape of the video rental industry. In 2000, **Netflix approached Blockbuster with an offer to be acquired for just $50 million**, but Blockbuster **turned them down multiple times**. In 2008, Blockbuster CEO Jim Keyes dismissed Netflix and Redbox as insignificant competitors. By the time Blockbuster attempted to replicate Netflix's digital model, it was too late. **Blockbuster went bankrupt, while Netflix grew into a multi-billion-dollar streaming giant.**

The consequences of status quo leadership are severe. Companies that fail to evolve risk talent drain, organizational stagnation, missed opportunities, and competitive disadvantage. Employees disengage when leaders provide no compelling vision for the future, leading to high turnover. Organizations that rely on reactive strategies fall behind their competitors and struggle to remain relevant in a rapidly changing business landscape.

In today's complex and fast-changing world, leadership cannot afford to be static or reactive. The future belongs to those who anticipate change, develop future leaders, and redefine business models to stay ahead of disruption. Leaders must shift from preserving the past to co-creating the future—or risk obsolescence. The choice is clear: remain trapped in the status quo and decline, or embrace proactive leadership and shape a thriving, resilient future.

This book is a manifesto for the quantum leader—the executive, entrepreneur, and decision-maker who recognizes that business as usual is no longer viable and that a new paradigm of leadership is required. It calls for leaders who move beyond traditional, linear thinking and embrace an interconnected, adaptive, and forward-thinking approach—one that fosters resilience, innovation, and long-term value creation in an era of constant transformation.

For leaders, this means embracing a proactive rather than reactive approach. Organizations must embed sustainability, innovation, and resilience into their business models, ensuring they are prepared for inevitable shifts rather than scrambling to adapt once disruption has already taken hold. Companies that fail to pivot will face obsolescence, while those that recognize the urgency of transformation will emerge as the pioneers of the next economic paradigm.

Reflection

5. The New Business Landscape: Adaptability and Interconnectedness

Adaptability is no longer a competitive advantage; it is the foundation of survival. Businesses that fail to anticipate and respond to rapid shifts in technology, consumer behavior, and regulatory landscapes will not just struggle—they will become relics of the past. Kodak dismissed digital photography, Blockbuster ignored streaming, and both paid the price. Meanwhile, AI and automation are redefining industries at an unprecedented pace, forcing leaders to cultivate agile decision-making, foresight, and a willingness to unlearn outdated models. In this new reality, rigid structures and incremental improvements are no longer enough—leaders must embrace continuous reinvention.

The days of fixed, five-year business plans are over. Success in this rapidly evolving environment is not about predicting the future with precision but about being prepared for multiple potential futures. This requires organizations to adopt fluidity, continuous iteration, and adaptive strategy development. A culture of experimentation, real-time data-driven decision-making, and decentralized leadership must replace outdated, hierarchical models. Companies that wait for certainty before acting will already be obsolete—the future belongs to those who move forward with conviction in the face of uncertainty.

Interconnectedness is the defining feature of the modern economy. No business operates in isolation. Supply chains span continents, economies are intertwined, and digital ecosystems bridge industries in ways unimaginable just a few decades ago. This means that businesses must shift from siloed operations to ecosystem thinking, recognizing that every decision—whether in sourcing, production, or investment—creates ripple effects across industries and societies. Leaders who fail to see this broader interconnected landscape will be blindsided by the cascading effects of their actions—or their inaction.

Companies must also recognize the power of collaboration over competition. In an era where disruption is constant, those who co-create solutions, share data, and engage in open innovation will find themselves at the forefront of the new business order. Strategic alliances, cross-sector partnerships, and knowledge-sharing networks will no longer be optional but essential for sustainable growth. Cirque du Soleil thrived not by competing within a dying industry but by reinventing it altogether. Similarly, the most forward-thinking organizations of today will not merely react to change but actively shape the future—creating new paradigms, industries, and opportunities that others struggle to follow.

Reflection

Chapter 2: The Quantum Business Paradigm

1. Introducing the Quantum Business Paradigm

The business world is no longer a predictable, linear system that responds to traditional strategic planning and control mechanisms. In the past, organizations relied on structured methodologies, hierarchical decision-making, and stable markets to drive predictable outcomes. However, today's global economy operates at an exponential pace, fueled by technological advancements, geopolitical shifts, and evolving consumer expectations. Businesses must contend with disruptive forces such as artificial intelligence (AI), automation, economic uncertainties, and environmental crises. Those that fail to adapt will face obsolescence, while those that embrace resilience, innovation, and conscious leadership will thrive.

The limitations of classical business thinking, rooted in industrial capitalism, are now evident. Classical models prioritized efficiency, resource optimization, and hierarchical control, which worked well in an environment with low variability and limited disruptions. However, the rise of the digital age, globalization, and automation introduced complexities that rigid business structures struggled to accommodate. The Fourth Industrial Revolution, characterized by AI, blockchain, and quantum computing, further disrupted traditional management principles. As businesses face a constant state of flux, leadership must shift from command-and-control models to adaptive, systems-based thinking.

The Quantum Business paradigm rejects the linear, deterministic approach of traditional capitalism, which views businesses as isolated entities focused solely on profit maximization. Instead, it embraces a holistic, interconnected perspective that considers the wider community, the environment, and the global economy. This shift acknowledges that every business decision creates ripple effects, much like the quantum concept of entanglement, where changes in one part of the system influence the whole.

For example, a manufacturing company that outsources production to a country with lax environmental regulations may experience short-term cost savings, but the long-term consequences—environmental degradation, health crises, and reputational damage—can erode consumer trust and investor confidence. Nike, for instance, faced significant backlash in the 1990s when reports surfaced about sweatshop conditions, child labor, and environmental neglect in its overseas factories. The resulting consumer protests and boycotts forced the company to overhaul its supply chain practices. Similarly, fast fashion brands like Zara and H&M have been criticized for outsourcing production to countries with weak environmental regulations, leading to water pollution, excessive waste, and hazardous working conditions. The 2013 Rana Plaza factory collapse in Bangladesh, which killed over 1,100 workers, exposed the devastating human and environmental costs of these practices. This interconnectedness, often unseen through a traditional business lens, becomes clear under the Quantum Business framework, which acknowledges that every business decision creates ripple effects that extend beyond immediate profitability to impact communities, ecosystems, and long-term sustainability. Another key shift in Quantum Business is the acceptance of uncertainty and dynamism. Traditional capitalism attempts to control market forces through rigid planning, forecasting models, and incremental improvements. However, in an era of continuous disruption, success is no longer about predicting the future perfectly but about being prepared for multiple potential futures.

The concept of superposition in quantum mechanics—where a particle exists in multiple states until observed—mirrors how businesses must embrace multiple possibilities simultaneously. Leaders must remain open to emerging trends, foster a culture of innovation, and continuously iterate their strategies rather than relying on outdated playbooks.

The failures of companies like Kodak and Blockbuster demonstrate the dangers of rigid, status quo leadership. Kodak invented the digital camera in 1975 but refused to embrace digital photography for fear of cannibalizing its film business. Similarly, Blockbuster dismissed Netflix's streaming model, failing to recognize the impending industry shift. Both companies collapsed as a result of their inability to adapt. Meanwhile, organizations like Netflix and Cirque du Soleil thrived by redefining their industries rather than resisting change.

In this new reality, profit maximization alone is insufficient. Companies must integrate profitability with purpose, intelligence with intuition, and ambition with ethical responsibility. The focus shifts from shareholder value to stakeholder value, encompassing employees, customers, communities, and the environment. Businesses that prioritize ethical governance, corporate responsibility, and sustainability will not only survive but lead the next economic evolution. For example, companies that once saw corporate social responsibility (CSR) as optional are now recognizing it as a fundamental driver of long-term success. The shift toward conscious capitalism is not just about philanthropy; it is about embedding sustainability, fairness, and ethical decision-making into business models. Organizations that adopt regenerative business models—which replenish environmental and social capital rather than depleting them—will shape the future of capitalism.

No business operates in isolation. Supply chains span continents, economies are intertwined, and digital ecosystems connect industries in ways unimaginable a few decades ago. Leaders must move from siloed operations to ecosystem thinking, recognizing that partnerships, data sharing, and cross-sector collaboration will define the future of sustainable growth. Companies that co-create solutions rather than compete in zero-sum games will emerge as leaders. The rise of platform economies, decentralized finance, and blockchain-based supply chains illustrates how businesses can leverage interconnected systems to create shared value rather than extract value.

The transition to Quantum Business requires a profound shift in leadership style. Leaders must move away from top-down control and embrace collaborative, trust-based decision-making. This demands emotional intelligence, mindfulness, and holistic decision-making that prioritizes the long-term impact of business choices rather than focusing on short-term financial gains. Businesses must develop adaptive strategies that enable them to pivot and iterate rather than resist change.

In quantum physics, the act of observing a system alters its state. Similarly, how leaders observe and engage with their teams, customers, and industries directly influences outcomes. The rise of mindful leadership, spiritual intelligence, and organizational well-being is not just a philosophical ideal—it is a practical necessity for businesses that want to thrive in complexity.

The traditional business model, shaped by industrial-era efficiency and hierarchical management, is no longer sustainable in a world defined by fluidity, complexity, and interdependence. The Quantum Business framework provides a more holistic, adaptive, and sustainable approach, ensuring that businesses remain resilient, innovative, and ethically grounded. To navigate this transformation, organizations must shift from rigid strategic planning to dynamic adaptation, embrace interconnected ecosystems rather than isolated operations, prioritize long-term value creation over short-term financial engineering, and foster a leadership culture based on trust, mindfulness, and ethical responsibility.

The future of business will be shaped by those who understand that success is no longer about control—it is about co-creation. The transition to Quantum Business requires courage, vision, and a commitment to transforming the very nature of capitalism. Those who embrace the principles of interconnectedness, uncertainty, and ethical leadership will lead us toward a more just, sustainable, and thriving global economy.

Reflection

2. The Imperative for Quantum Leadership

As we discussed in the last chapter, the business world is no longer a predictable, linear system governed by traditional strategic planning and control mechanisms. The Quantum Business paradigm rejects the deterministic approach of classical capitalism, which views businesses as isolated entities focused solely on profit maximization. Instead, it embraces a holistic, interconnected perspective that acknowledges the complexities of today's global economy. Organizations must now navigate disruptive forces such as artificial intelligence, automation, economic uncertainties, and environmental crises. Those that fail to adapt will face obsolescence, while those that embrace resilience, innovation, and conscious leadership will thrive.

The limitations of classical business thinking, rooted in industrial capitalism, are now evident. Traditional models prioritized efficiency, resource optimization, and hierarchical control, which worked well in an environment with limited variability. However, the rise of the digital age, globalization, and automation introduced complexities that rigid business structures struggled to accommodate. The Fourth Industrial Revolution, characterized by AI, blockchain, and quantum computing, has further disrupted conventional management principles. Leaders must now transition from command-and-control models to adaptive, systems-based thinking to remain competitive in a rapidly evolving landscape.

The Imperative of Quantum Leadership

At the heart of Quantum Business is Quantum Leadership—an approach that acknowledges the interconnected nature of modern organizations. Today's businesses do not operate in isolation; they exist within interdependent networks of stakeholders, global markets, supply chains, and technological ecosystems. This reality necessitates a shift from siloed decision-making to systems thinking. Quantum Leaders understand that every decision ripples across multiple dimensions, requiring the ability to synthesize vast amounts of information, anticipate second-order consequences, and respond proactively.

Moreover, Quantum Leadership recognizes that innovation is not a top-down initiative but an emergent property of a well-orchestrated system. Instead of relying on rigid innovation pipelines, Quantum Leaders cultivate environments of continuous learning and experimentation. They foster adaptive cultures where breakthrough solutions emerge organically through cross-functional collaborations and external partnerships. True innovation often arises from unexpected intersections of disciplines, industries, and perspectives, and Quantum Leaders are skilled at nurturing these creative collisions.

The Human-Centric Approach to Leadership

In an age increasingly dominated by automation and artificial intelligence, the most valuable asset of any organization remains its people. Quantum Business prioritizes a human-centric approach, where leadership is driven by purpose, ethical decision-making, and holistic well-being. Sustainable success is no longer defined by short-term profit maximization but by cultivating engaged, purpose-driven teams. Quantum Leaders recognize their role as stewards of organizational ecosystems, balancing economic imperatives with societal and environmental responsibilities. Rather than operating with a purely transactional mindset, they foster relationships built on trust, authenticity, and ethical governance.

Heart-centered leadership is not a soft concept; it is a strategic necessity. Employees, consumers, and stakeholders increasingly demand authenticity, ethical leadership, and a commitment to values beyond profit. Organizations that cultivate a culture of purpose, well-being, and collective prosperity will attract top talent, foster deep customer loyalty, and establish lasting competitive advantages.

The Evolution of Leadership: From Authority to Empowerment

The leadership paradigm is shifting from authoritative command-and-control models to Quantum Leadership, which emphasizes empowerment, inspiration, and co-creation. The leaders of the future will not dictate from the top but will foster collaborative decision-making, nurture innovation, and instill trust within their teams. This requires a deep understanding of self, others, and the broader world—qualities that stem from conscious awareness and emotional intelligence (EI).

Leaders with high EI can navigate complex relationships, manage conflicts, and create a positive and motivated workplace culture. They inspire teams, build trust, and cultivate environments where collaboration and innovation thrive. Furthermore, a strong commitment to planetary and societal well-being will be essential. Businesses no longer operate in isolation; future leaders must take responsibility for their organizations' impact, prioritizing sustainability, ethical practices, and social responsibility to ensure long-term success.

The quantum age of business calls for a new kind of leadership—one that harmonizes data-driven intelligence with deep human wisdom. The traditional corporate playbook, which prioritized efficiency and bottom-line results at any cost, is no longer sufficient. The leaders who will shape the future are those who operate with conscious awareness, emotional intelligence, and a commitment to planetary and societal well-being. By embracing the principles of Quantum Business, leaders can drive meaningful impact, balancing stability with flexibility, vision with adaptability, and profit with purpose. The next era of business leadership belongs to those who can navigate complexity with agility, foster innovation with openness, and lead with both heart and strategy. In doing so, they will not only future-proof their organizations but also contribute to a more sustainable, ethical, and human-centered global economy.

Reflection

Chapter 3: Conscious Decision-Making and Leadership

1. The Role of Conscious Leadership

The transition to a truly quantum business model hinges on a fundamental shift in leadership—a move from the traditional, often transactional, approach to one characterized by conscious leadership. This isn't merely about adopting a new set of management techniques; it's a profound transformation of mindset, values, and behaviors. Conscious leaders understand that their role extends far beyond profit maximization; they see themselves as stewards of their organizations and agents of positive change in the world.

Self-awareness is the cornerstone of conscious leadership. These leaders possess a deep understanding of their own strengths, weaknesses, values, and biases. They are acutely aware of their emotional state and how their actions impact others. This self-knowledge allows them to make conscious choices, aligning their behavior with their values and avoiding the pitfalls of ego-driven decision-making. This isn't about narcissistic self-absorption; rather, it's a grounded understanding of self that informs them of their interactions with others and their approach to business challenges. A leader lacking self-awareness risks making decisions based on fear, insecurity, or personal agendas, undermining the holistic and interconnected approach crucial to a quantum business model.

Empathy is another critical quality of conscious leaders. They possess the ability to understand and share the feelings of others, both within their organizations and in the broader community. They actively listen to the concerns and perspectives of their employees, customers, and other stakeholders, fostering a culture of trust and collaboration. This empathetic understanding is not merely a soft skill; it's a strategic imperative, allowing leaders to anticipate needs, address potential conflicts proactively, and build stronger relationships with all stakeholders. A leader lacking empathy risks creating a toxic work environment, alienating customers, and damaging their organization's reputation. They fail to appreciate the interconnectedness of their actions and their impact on the wider ecosystem.

Integrity is the bedrock of trust and ethical decision-making. Conscious leaders act in accordance with their values, even when it's difficult or challenging. They prioritize ethical conduct over short-term gains, understanding that long-term sustainability depends on building a reputation of honesty and trustworthiness. This integrity extends to all aspects of their business operations, from supply chain management and environmental practices to interactions with employees and customers. A leader lacking integrity risks eroding trust, undermining their organization's reputation, and potentially facing severe legal or ethical repercussions. The interconnectedness of actions means that a lack of integrity in one area can ripple through the entire organization and its surrounding ecosystem.

Furthermore, conscious leaders are driven by a purpose that transcends personal gain. They understand that their work has a broader impact on the world and strive to create positive changes through their business activities. This sense of purpose provides them with resilience, motivation, and a clear compass in navigating complex challenges. They see their organization not just as a profit-generating machine but as a vehicle for social good, contributing to the well-being of the community and the environment. A leader without this sense of purpose often falls prey to short-sighted decision-making, neglecting long-term sustainability and the holistic interconnectedness of their actions.

Several examples illustrate these qualities in action. Consider Patagonia, a company renowned for its commitment to environmental sustainability. Its founder, Yvon Chouinard, embodies conscious leadership through his unwavering dedication to environmental protection and his commitment to ethical business practices. Patagonia's actions—from its use of recycled materials to its advocacy for environmental conservation—demonstrate a profound understanding of interconnectedness and a commitment to serving a higher purpose. Their success exemplifies the fact that a focus on purpose doesn't necessarily preclude profitability; in fact, it often enhances it by fostering customer loyalty and attracting talented employees. Another example is TOMS Shoes, a company known for its "One for One" model, where for every pair of shoes purchased, a pair is donated to a child in need. Blake Mycoskie, the founder, demonstrates conscious leadership by prioritizing social impact alongside profitability. This approach creates a powerful brand narrative, attracting customers who are drawn to the company's mission and values. TOMS Shoes show how aligning business goals with a larger social purpose can be a powerful engine for growth and positive social change.

These examples highlight that conscious leadership is not merely an idealistic aspiration; it's a practical approach to business that can yield both financial success and profound positive impact. It requires a shift in mindset from a purely transactional view of business to a relational perspective, recognizing the intricate web of interconnectedness between the business, its employees, its customers, its community, and the environment. Developing conscious leadership qualities requires a multifaceted approach. It involves self-reflection, ongoing earning, and the cultivation of specific skills such as emotional intelligence, mindfulness, and systems thinking.

Leadership development programs designed to foster these qualities are crucial for creating a new generation of business leaders who are capable of navigating the complexities of the modern world. These programs shouldn't just focus on traditional business skills; they must also incorporate practices that promote self-awareness, emotional intelligence, and a sense of purpose. This might involve incorporating mindfulness techniques, ethical frameworks, and exercises designed to foster empathy and collaboration.

Furthermore, creating a culture of conscious leadership requires a commitment from the top down. Leaders must model the behavior they expect from their teams, creating an environment where ethical conduct, sustainability, and social responsibility are valued and rewarded. This requires a conscious effort to foster open communication, trust, and a shared understanding of the organization's purpose. Incentive structures should reflect these values, recognizing and rewarding contributions that go beyond simply maximizing profit.

The transition to a conscious leadership model is not a quick fix; it's a journey of continuous learning and evolution. It requires a willingness to embrace vulnerability, to learn from mistakes, and to continuously adapt and improve. But the rewards are immense: a more engaged and motivated workforce, stronger relationships with customers and stakeholders, and a more meaningful contribution to the world. This approach ultimately contributes to the broader transition toward a quantum business model, a model that recognizes the interconnectedness of all things and prioritizes both profit and purpose. By cultivating conscious leadership, businesses can pave the way for a more sustainable, equitable, and fulfilling future for all.

The journey towards conscious capitalism requires vision, courage, and a deep commitment to a fundamentally different way of doing business—a way that prioritizes the well-being of all stakeholders, and recognizes that the true measure of success is not simply profit, but positive impact.

Reflection

2. Conscious Decision-Making: The Art of Intentional Choices

Conscious decision-making is the process of making choices with full awareness, careful thought, and deliberate intention. Unlike automatic or impulsive decision-making, which is often driven by habits, emotions, or unconscious biases, conscious decision-making requires individuals to assess their options, consider the consequences, and align their choices with their values and goals. This process plays a crucial role in personal and professional life, allowing people to navigate complex situations, improve problem-solving, and achieve desired outcomes.

At its core, conscious decision-making involves mindfulness, critical thinking, and self-awareness. Instead of making choices on autopilot, individuals actively engage their cognitive faculties to evaluate different possibilities and their potential impact. This type of decision-making includes several key components:

- **Awareness**: Recognizing that a decision needs to be made and acknowledging the factors influencing it.
- **Evaluation**: Analyzing the available information, considering alternatives, and weighing the pros and cons.
- **Intention**: Ensuring that decisions align with long-term objectives, ethical principles, and core values.
- **Action**: Taking deliberate steps based on informed choices and accepting accountability for the outcomes.

- Action
- Intention
- Evaluation
- Awareness

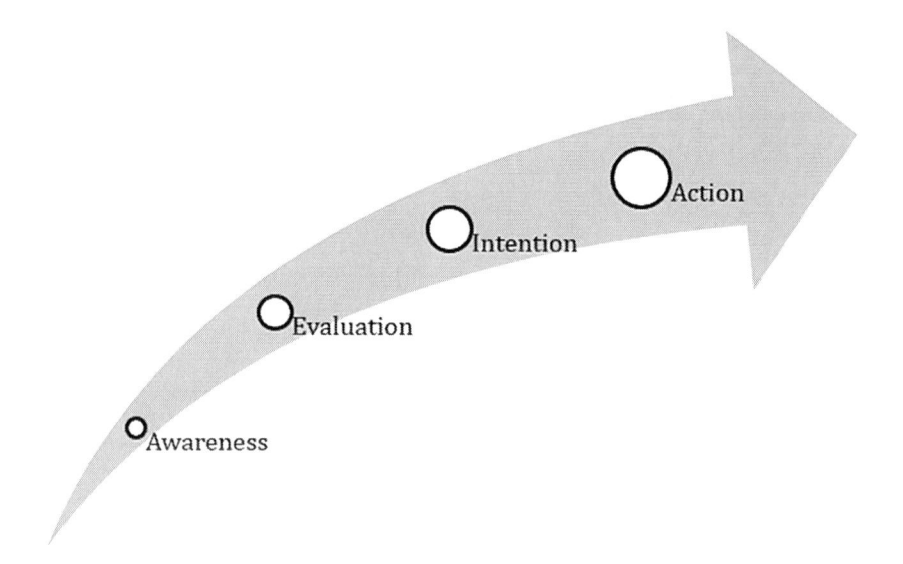

Steps in Conscious Decision Making

By practicing conscious decision-making, individuals can improve their ability to respond effectively to challenges and opportunities rather than reacting impulsively based on emotions or external pressures.

The Role of Self-Awareness in Conscious Decision-Making

Self-awareness is a fundamental aspect of conscious decision-making. It allows individuals to understand their thoughts, emotions, and motivations, helping them make choices that align with their personal values and goals. People who practice self-awareness can recognize cognitive biases, emotional influences, and external pressures that may distort their judgment.

For example, someone making a career decision might consider their long-term aspirations, personal strengths, and work-life balance rather than simply following societal expectations or immediate financial incentives. By being aware of their priorities, they can make choices that lead to greater fulfillment and success in the long run.

Emotional Intelligence and Conscious Decision-Making

Emotional intelligence plays a significant role in conscious decision-making by helping individuals manage their emotions and understand the emotions of others. High emotional intelligence enables people to remain calm under pressure, regulate impulsive reactions, and make rational decisions that take into account both logic and empathy.

For instance, in conflict resolution, a person with strong emotional intelligence will consciously choose their words and actions to de-escalate the situation rather than reacting aggressively or defensively. This ability to navigate emotional complexities allows for better personal and professional relationships.

Conscious decision-making is a critical skill for leaders and individuals navigating an increasingly complex world. By cultivating self-awareness, emotional intelligence, and intentionality, individuals can make informed, ethical, and strategic choices that contribute to personal growth and professional success. The integration of conscious decision-making into leadership practices enables organizations to foster a culture of responsibility, innovation, and meaningful impact. In a rapidly evolving business environment, the ability to make thoughtful, intentional decisions will set leaders apart, allowing them to navigate uncertainty with clarity and confidence.

Reflection

3. Leading with Empathy and Emotional Intelligence

Building upon the foundation of purpose-driven leadership and the principles of interconnectedness, we now delve into the critical role of empathy and emotional intelligence in cultivating a truly conscious business. While establishing a clear organizational purpose and fostering a sense of belonging are vital first steps, translating these intentions into tangible action requires a deep understanding of human dynamics. This understanding is precisely where empathy and emotional intelligence become indispensable assets.

Empathy, the capacity to understand and share the feelings of another, is not merely a soft skill; it is the bedrock of effective leadership in a conscious organization. It is about stepping into the shoes of employees, understanding their perspectives, and acknowledging their emotions, both positive and negative. This does not mean agreeing with every sentiment expressed but rather creating a space where feelings are validated and understood. In a business setting, this means actively listening to employees' concerns, anxieties, and aspirations. It means acknowledging the challenges they face, both professional and personal, and providing support wherever possible. Consider, for example, a manager facing a team member struggling with burnout. A leader lacking empathy might simply focus on meeting deadlines and increasing productivity, potentially exacerbating the situation. An empathetic leader, however, would take the time to understand the root causes of the burnout, perhaps discovering personal stressors affecting the employee's performance. This understanding might lead to offering flexible work arrangements, providing additional support, or even suggesting professional help. The result? A more engaged, productive, and loyal employee, and a stronger, more resilient team.

Emotional intelligence, a broader concept encompassing self-awareness, self-regulation, social awareness, and relationship management, complements and amplifies the power of empathy. Self-awareness, the ability to understand one's own emotions and their impact on others, is crucial for leaders. A self-aware leader recognizes their own biases, limitations, and emotional triggers, enabling them to manage their reactions and communicate more effectively. This prevents impulsive decisions based on personal feelings, ensuring objectivity in critical situations. Self-regulation, the ability to control and manage one's emotions, is equally important. Leaders who can remain calm and composed under pressure, even during challenging conversations, create a sense of stability and security for their team. This allows for more constructive dialogue, even when dealing with conflict or difficult situations. For instance, a leader facing criticism from a client might instinctively become defensive. However, a leader with strong self-regulation would take a moment to process their emotions, respond thoughtfully, and address the concerns in a professional and respectful manner.

Social awareness, the ability to understand and respond appropriately to the emotions of others, is directly linked to empathy. It involves observing body language, listening actively to verbal cues, and interpreting unspoken emotions. This awareness is essential for building strong relationships, fostering collaboration, and resolving conflicts constructively. In a diverse workplace, social awareness is particularly critical, enabling leaders to navigate cultural differences and ensure inclusivity.

Finally, relationship management, the ability to build and maintain positive relationships, utilizes all the previous components. It involves actively fostering collaboration, resolving conflicts constructively, and building trust within the team. This goes beyond simply managing tasks; it is about cultivating genuine connections with employees, creating a supportive and collaborative environment.

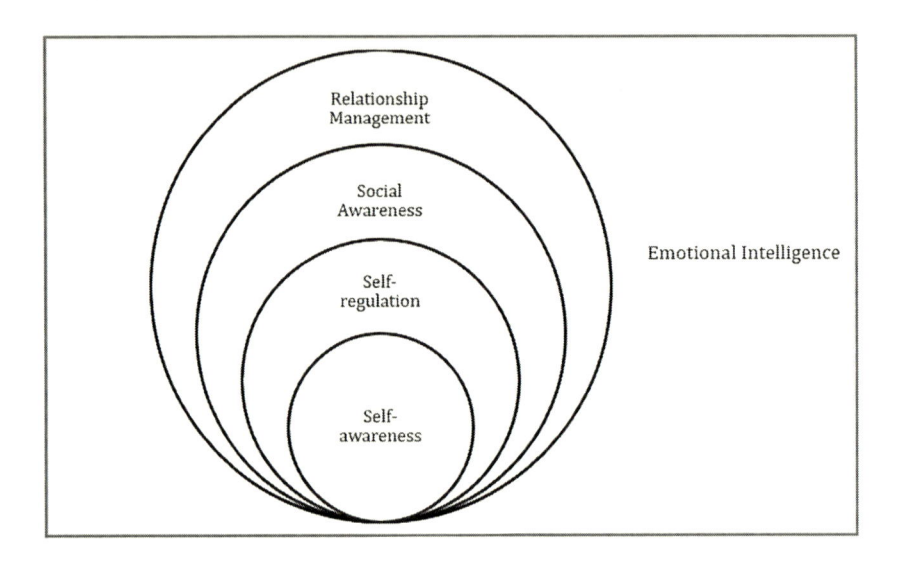

```
                    Relationship
                    Management

                  Social
                  Awareness
                                              Emotional Intelligence
                Self-
                regulation

              Self-
              awareness
```

The investment in nurturing empathy and emotional intelligence is not merely a cost; it is a strategic investment that yields substantial returns in terms of employee engagement, retention, innovation, and overall organizational effectiveness. Effective leadership requires more than vision and strategic execution; it demands the ability to connect, understand, and uplift those within the organization. As businesses evolve towards a more conscious and interconnected model, integrating empathy and emotional intelligence into leadership practices will be essential for sustainable success. By prioritizing these principles, organizations can cultivate a resilient, purpose-driven culture that thrives on mutual trust, collaboration, and shared success.

Reflection

4. Benefits of Conscious Decision-Making

Practicing conscious decision-making leads to several benefits. One of the primary advantages is improved problem-solving, as individuals who carefully evaluate all factors can find more effective and creative solutions to challenges. Another key benefit is increased confidence since making deliberate, well-informed choices fosters self-trust and confidence in one's abilities.

Conscious decision-making also reduces regret and anxiety. When individuals make thoughtful choices, they are less likely to experience remorse over impulsive actions that may have led to negative consequences. Additionally, conscious decision-making strengthens personal and professional relationships by enhancing communication, empathy, and trust in interactions with others. Finally, this practice ensures alignment with personal goals and values, allowing individuals to stay true to their long-term aspirations and ethical principles.

Reflection

5. Challenges in Conscious Decision-Making

Despite its benefits, conscious decision-making can be challenging. One major obstacle is cognitive bias, which refers to the natural tendency of humans to favor certain viewpoints. Examples include confirmation bias, where individuals favor information that supports their existing beliefs, and anchoring bias, where the first piece of information received heavily influences decision-making.

Another challenge is information overload. In today's digital age, individuals are often overwhelmed with excessive amounts of data, making it difficult to filter relevant details for decision-making. Time constraints also pose a challenge, as making conscious decisions requires careful thought and effort, which may not always be available in fast-paced environments.

Emotional triggers can further cloud judgment and lead to impulsive decisions. Strong emotions such as stress, fear, or excitement can prevent individuals from thinking rationally. Additionally, social pressures may push individuals toward making decisions that do not align with their values or best interests, whether from peers, cultural expectations, or authority figures.

Overcoming these challenges requires mindfulness, patience, and a commitment to ongoing self-reflection and learning.

Reflection

6. How to Develop Conscious Decision-Making Skills

Improving conscious decision-making is a skill that can be cultivated through practice and discipline. One effective approach is practicing mindfulness, which involves being present and aware of one's thoughts, emotions, and surroundings. Mindfulness helps individuals slow down and make more intentional choices.

Asking critical questions is another useful technique. Before making a decision, individuals should ask themselves questions such as: What are my options? What are the possible outcomes? How does this align with my values and goals? These questions help clarify thoughts and prevent hasty choices.

Gathering and evaluating information is essential in conscious decision-making. Taking the time to research, analyze facts, and seek different perspectives ensures that decisions are based on reliable information. Managing emotions is equally important, as individuals must recognize when their emotions are influencing their decisions and take a step back to reflect before acting.

Using decision-making frameworks can also enhance conscious decision-making. Tools such as cost-benefit analysis, the Eisenhower Matrix, or the SMART criteria provide structured ways to approach choices and ensure logical reasoning. Seeking feedback from trusted mentors, colleagues, or friends can provide valuable insights and help individuals reduce bias in their decision-making.

By applying these techniques consistently, individuals can develop the habit of making thoughtful, well-informed decisions that lead to positive outcomes. Conscious decision-making is a powerful skill that allows individuals to make choices with awareness, clarity, and intention. By integrating self-awareness, critical thinking, and emotional intelligence into their decision-making process, people can improve their ability to solve problems, strengthen relationships, and align their choices with their long-term goals. Although challenges such as cognitive biases, information overload, and emotional influences can interfere with decision-making, practicing mindfulness, seeking diverse perspectives, and using structured decision-making frameworks can help overcome these obstacles. In a world where individuals are constantly faced with choices, developing conscious decision-making skills is essential for personal growth, professional success, and overall well-being.

Reflection

7. Moving from Linear Decision-Making to Quantum Business Thinking

At the heart of *Quantum Business* is the understanding that reality is not linear, siloed, or static—it is relational, dynamic, and co-created. This worldview invites decision-makers to shift from deterministic, either/or thinking to a more expansive, both/and perspective. Here, conscious decision-making is not just a skill but a way of *being*—a state of awareness where leaders recognize themselves as active participants in a greater field of energy, meaning, and possibility.

1. Mindfulness as Quantum Presence

Mindfulness, as discussed in Section 6, is foundational—but in *quantum terms*, it becomes *quantum presence*—the capacity to attune to the present moment while simultaneously sensing the energetic field around a decision. In this state, leaders learn to perceive subtle cues, patterns, and synchronicities. This isn't just about being "aware" but being vibrationally aligned with one's inner knowing and the larger systemic intelligence. Decisions are no longer reactive—they are emergent.

2. Asking Critical Questions as a Portal to Multidimensional Inquiry

Quantum decision-makers go beyond surface-level questions to inquire from multiple dimensions: the logical, the intuitive, the emotional, and the ethical. When one asks, "How does this align with my values and goals?"—a quantum thinker adds, "How does this align with the greater good? What field of possibility does this decision open up? What is the subtle message life is offering me here?" This expands the field of inquiry into one that is integrative and ethically aware.

3. Evaluating Information Through Energetic Discernment

Traditional models emphasize gathering facts; *quantum discernment* includes sensing the *quality* of information. Is this data coming from a fear-based narrative or from a possibility-based consciousness? What voices are missing from this conversation? Quantum decision-making values the coherence of perspectives, inviting diverse viewpoints and honoring silence as much as speech—an attunement to the unseen as much as the seen.

4. Managing Emotions Through Coherence, Not Suppression

In classical decision-making, emotions are often viewed as liabilities. In quantum business, emotions are information—they are energetic signatures that can guide or mislead depending on the level of coherence. Through coherence practices like breathwork, heart-centered reflection, and somatic intelligence, leaders learn to harness emotional signals as integral inputs rather than distractions.

5. Frameworks that Reflect the Quantum Nature of Reality

Linear tools like SMART goals or Eisenhower Matrices are helpful, but quantum business thinking calls for *dynamic frameworks*—such as polarity mapping, systemic constellation work, and the use of narrative intelligence. These tools acknowledge that decision-making happens in a living system with multiple interdependencies, and the act of observing a problem can itself transform the solution.

6. Seeking Feedback as Collective Co-Creation

Rather than merely seeking advice, quantum leaders engage in *conscious co-creation*. Feedback is received as an act of mutual awakening—an opportunity to mirror blind spots, amplify potential, and catalyze evolution. This is not a mechanical feedback loop but a relational, humanistic engagement rooted in trust, resonance, and shared purpose.

Section 6 presents essential practices—mindfulness, critical inquiry, emotional regulation, information analysis, and frameworks for rational thinking. These serve as the *entry point*. Quantum business reframes and expands them, anchoring these techniques in a deeper awareness of *consciousness itself*—the creative source from which all decisions emerge. Thus, quantum decision-making becomes an act of alignment—aligning the self with purpose, the system with integrity, and the moment with potential. When leaders cultivate this level of presence and awareness, decisions are no longer just *made*—they are *revealed*.

Reflection

Chapter 4: Critical Thinking and Ethical Leadership

1. Critical Thinking: The Foundation of Effective Decision-Making

Critical thinking is the ability to analyze, evaluate, and interpret information objectively to form a reasoned judgment. It is a fundamental skill that enables individuals to make well-informed decisions, solve complex problems, and navigate the vast amount of information encountered daily. Unlike passive thinking, which involves accepting information at face value, critical thinking requires questioning assumptions, identifying biases, and weighing evidence before reaching conclusions.

In today's rapidly changing world, critical thinking is more important than ever. Whether in education, business, healthcare, or everyday decision-making, the ability to think critically allows individuals to assess situations logically and make choices based on sound reasoning rather than emotions or external influences.

Reflection

2. Understanding Critical Thinking

Critical thinking is a disciplined and systematic way of processing information to make rational and well-informed decisions. It involves various cognitive skills and intellectual behaviors, including analysis, interpretation, inference, explanation, and self-regulation. These skills enable individuals to evaluate information critically rather than simply accepting it as true.

One of the fundamental aspects of critical thinking is **analysis**. This involves breaking down complex ideas into smaller parts to understand their meaning and significance. Analytical thinking allows individuals to differentiate between relevant and irrelevant information, identify key arguments, and recognize patterns or connections between concepts.

Interpretation is another crucial aspect of critical thinking. It involves understanding and clarifying the meaning of information, whether it is in the form of written text, verbal communication, data, or visual content. A critical thinker can accurately interpret the intended message of an argument, distinguish between fact and opinion, and assess the credibility of sources.

Inference refers to the ability to draw logical conclusions based on available evidence. Critical thinkers use inference to predict possible outcomes, evaluate potential consequences, and identify underlying assumptions. Instead of relying on gut feelings or assumptions, they use logic and reason to make sound judgments.

Another essential component of critical thinking is **explanation**. A critical thinker can clearly articulate their reasoning, present evidence to support their conclusions, and defend their viewpoint against opposing arguments. Effective communication of ideas is an important aspect of critical thinking, especially in academic, professional, and social settings.

Finally, **self-regulation** is a key characteristic of critical thinking. This involves being aware of one's own cognitive biases, examining personal beliefs, and adjusting one's thinking based on new information. Self-regulation allows individuals to remain open-minded, consider alternative viewpoints, and refine their reasoning over time.

Reflection

3. The Importance of Critical Thinking

Critical thinking plays a crucial role in various aspects of life, from personal decision-making to professional success. It enables individuals to make logical and rational choices, solve problems effectively, and approach complex issues with clarity and objectivity.

In **education**, critical thinking is essential for developing analytical and reasoning skills. Students who practice critical thinking can evaluate different perspectives, understand complex concepts, and engage in meaningful discussions. Instead of passively memorizing information, they learn to question assumptions, seek evidence, and develop independent thought. Critical thinking also helps students become better writers, researchers, and debaters, as they can construct well-reasoned arguments and critically assess the validity of sources.

In **business and leadership**, critical thinking is an invaluable skill that contributes to effective decision-making and problem-solving. Business leaders must analyze market trends, assess risks, and make strategic decisions that impact their organizations. Without critical thinking, they may fall victim to cognitive biases, misinformation, or flawed reasoning. Companies that encourage critical thinking among employees foster innovation, creativity, and adaptability, allowing them to thrive in competitive environments.

In **healthcare and medicine**, critical thinking is vital for diagnosing illnesses, evaluating treatment options, and ensuring patient safety. Doctors, nurses, and medical professionals must assess symptoms, interpret test results, and make informed decisions based on scientific evidence. A lack of critical thinking in healthcare can lead to misdiagnoses, medical errors, and ineffective treatments. Healthcare practitioners who apply critical thinking can provide better patient care, reduce risks, and improve health outcomes.

In **everyday life**, critical thinking helps individuals navigate misinformation, make better financial decisions, and resolve conflicts. In an age of social media and digital information, people are constantly exposed to biased news, misleading advertisements, and propaganda. Critical thinking enables individuals to fact-check information, recognize logical fallacies, and make informed decisions rather than being easily influenced by emotions or external pressures.

Reflection

4. Challenges in Developing Critical Thinking

Despite its importance, developing strong critical thinking skills can be challenging. Several obstacles can hinder an individual's ability to think critically, including cognitive biases, emotional influences, and social conditioning.

One of the most common barriers to critical thinking is **cognitive bias**. People naturally tend to favor information that confirms their existing beliefs while ignoring or dismissing contradictory evidence. This phenomenon, known as confirmation bias, prevents individuals from considering alternative viewpoints and leads to distorted reasoning. Other biases, such as anchoring bias (relying too heavily on initial information) and hindsight bias (believing past events were predictable), can also affect judgment.

Emotional reasoning is another challenge in critical thinking. People often make decisions based on emotions rather than logic. Fear, anger, excitement, or frustration can cloud judgment and lead to irrational choices. For example, someone may react impulsively in a conflict rather than considering the best course of action. Learning to separate emotions from logic is a key aspect of developing critical thinking skills.

Social and cultural influences also play a role in shaping how people think. From an early age, individuals are exposed to societal norms, traditions, and authority figures that influence their beliefs and values. While cultural perspectives are valuable, blindly accepting traditions without questioning their validity can limit critical thinking. Encouraging open-mindedness and intellectual curiosity helps individuals develop a broader and more informed perspective.

Lack of proper education and training in critical thinking is another challenge. Traditional education systems often emphasize rote memorization and standardized testing rather than teaching students how to analyze, evaluate, and question information. Incorporating critical thinking exercises, debates, and problem-solving activities into educational curriculums can help students develop these essential skills.

Reflection

5. How to Improve Critical Thinking Skills

Developing critical thinking requires practice, self-awareness, and a willingness to challenge one's own assumptions. There are several strategies individuals can use to enhance their critical thinking abilities.

One effective strategy is **asking questions**. Critical thinkers regularly ask questions such as: What evidence supports this claim? Are there alternative explanations? What are the potential biases in this information? By questioning information rather than accepting it at face value, individuals can develop a more analytical mindset.

Another useful approach is **engaging in active learning**. Reading widely, participating in discussions, and seeking diverse perspectives help individuals expand their knowledge and improve their reasoning skills. Exposure to different viewpoints encourages open-mindedness and allows individuals to consider multiple angles of an issue.

Practicing logical reasoning is also essential. Engaging in activities such as puzzles, brain teasers, and logical reasoning exercises can sharpen analytical skills and enhance problem-solving abilities. Learning about logical fallacies, such as ad hominem attacks or false dilemmas, can also help individuals recognize flawed arguments and improve their ability to construct sound reasoning.

Seeking feedback is another important aspect of improving critical thinking. Engaging in discussions with peers, mentors, or experts allows individuals to receive constructive criticism and refine their reasoning. Being open to feedback helps individuals identify weaknesses in their thought processes and develop stronger analytical skills.

Finally, **cultivating self-awareness** is crucial. Recognizing personal biases, emotions, and thought patterns allows individuals to regulate their reasoning and make more objective decisions. Keeping a reflective journal, practicing mindfulness, or engaging in self-assessment exercises can help individuals develop greater self-awareness and improve their critical thinking abilities.

Critical thinking is a fundamental skill that enables individuals to analyze information, evaluate arguments, and make well-reasoned decisions. It plays a crucial role in education, business, healthcare, and daily life, allowing individuals to navigate complex situations with logic and clarity. Despite challenges such as cognitive biases, emotional influences, and social conditioning, critical thinking can be developed through questioning, active learning, logical reasoning, and self-awareness. In a world filled with misinformation, complexity, and uncertainty, the ability to think critically is essential for making informed decisions and achieving success in all aspects of life.

Critical thinking is another essential element of conscious decision-making. It enables individuals to analyze information objectively, question assumptions, and evaluate evidence before reaching a conclusion. Rather than making snap judgments, critical thinkers consider multiple perspectives and assess the validity of their sources of information.

In business, leaders who employ critical thinking can make more effective strategic decisions by analyzing market trends, assessing risks, and considering the long-term impact of their choices. Similarly, in personal life, people who think critically can make better financial, health, and relationship decisions by carefully considering the available options.

Reflection

Chapter 5: The Intersection of Business, Spirituality, and Purpose

1. Integrating Spirituality and Business

Integrating spirituality into the business world might seem like a radical departure from the traditional profit-driven model, a juxtaposition of seemingly disparate worlds.

However, a closer examination reveals a powerful synergy between spiritual principles and effective business practices. This isn't about imposing religious dogma on employees or creating a company prayer group; rather, it's about incorporating core spiritual values – mindfulness, compassion, interconnectedness, and a sense of purpose – to cultivate a more ethical, sustainable, and ultimately, successful enterprise.

The core of this approach lies in recognizing the inherent interconnectedness of all things. Traditional business models often operate under a fragmented worldview, viewing the organization as a separate entity from its employees, customers, community, and the environment. This siloed approach often leads to exploitative practices, ethical compromises, and a disregard for the long-term consequences of actions. A spiritually infused approach, however, acknowledges the interdependence of all stakeholders. Decisions are made not solely based on short-term profit maximization but with consideration for their ripple effects on the entire system. This holistic perspective fosters a sense of shared responsibility and collaboration, leading to more sustainable and equitable outcomes.

Mindfulness, a cornerstone of many spiritual traditions, plays a critical role in conscious business. It encourages present-moment awareness, allowing leaders and employees alike to make more informed and deliberate decisions. Instead of reacting impulsively to challenges, mindful individuals pause, reflect, and consider the implications of their actions before acting. This heightened self-awareness extends to emotional regulation, reducing stress, improving communication, and fostering a more harmonious work environment. In a fast-paced business world, mindfulness can be a powerful antidote to burnout and a catalyst for enhanced productivity and creativity. Companies that incorporate mindfulness practices, such as meditation or yoga, often experience improvements in employee well-being, reduce absenteeism, and increase job satisfaction. Supporting this, research on workplace Yoga interventions has shown a moderate and statistically significant effect in reducing work-related stress, underscoring their value as an effective, evidence-based strategy for promoting mental well-being in organizational settings (Della Valle et al., 2020).

Compassion, another essential spiritual principle, translates into empathy and understanding in the business context. Conscious leaders cultivate a deep sense of empathy for their employees, recognizing their individual needs and aspirations. They create a workplace where individuals feel valued, respected, and supported. Notably, research shows that practicing managers conceptualize compassion both as receivers and givers, highlighting the dual perspective essential for fostering a truly compassionate organization. Excessive focus on short-term goals can suppress compassion, while empathetic leadership serves as a vital enabler, helping to break vicious cycles and build virtuous ones (Banker & Bahl, 2018). This empathetic approach extends to customers and the wider community, leading to stronger relationships, increased customer loyalty, and a positive brand image. Companies demonstrating genuine compassion often attract and retain top talent, fostering a culture of collaboration and innovation. They are also more likely to respond effectively to societal needs, contributing to the well-being of the community they serve. This doesn't necessarily mean sacrificing profits; in fact, studies show that companies prioritizing ethical and compassionate practices often experience greater long-term financial success.

The concept of interconnectedness, central to many spiritual belief systems, is crucial for building sustainable and responsible businesses. It involves recognizing the interdependence of the organization with its environment and the wider community. This understanding leads to a commitment to environmental sustainability, ethical sourcing, and fair labor practices. Companies adopting this perspective invest in renewable energy, reduce their carbon footprint, and promote responsible consumption. They also prioritize fair trade practices, ensuring that their supply chains are ethical and sustainable. This commitment to interconnectedness is not just a feel-good exercise; it's a strategic imperative for long-term success in an increasingly conscious and environmentally aware world. Consumers are increasingly demanding transparency and accountability from businesses, and those embracing interconnectedness are better positioned to meet this demand.

Purpose, a powerful driver for both individuals and organizations, plays a vital role in conscious business. Moving beyond mere profit maximization, purpose-driven businesses define their mission in terms of a larger social or environmental good. They strive to make a positive impact on the world, aligning their operations with their values and contributing to the well-being of society. This sense of purpose provides a strong foundation for employee engagement, attracting and retaining individuals who are passionate about the company's mission. It also enhances brand loyalty and creates a powerful connection with customers who share those values. This approach often leads to greater innovation and creativity, as employees feel a sense of purpose and meaning in their work.

Integrating spirituality into business, however, isn't without its challenges. Some might argue that spirituality is a personal matter that shouldn't be imposed on the workplace. Others may express concern about the potential for religious bias or the blurring of lines between professional and personal life. These concerns are valid and need to be addressed thoughtfully. The key is to focus on the universal principles of mindfulness, compassion, interconnectedness, and purpose, rather than on any specific religious or spiritual tradition. Creating a culture of respect and inclusiveness is paramount, ensuring that all employees feel comfortable and valued regardless of their beliefs.

Moreover, implementing these principles requires a conscious effort from leadership. Leaders must model the desired behaviors, fostering an environment of trust, transparency, and open communication. They must create systems and structures that support ethical decision-making, sustainable practices, and social responsibility. This involves developing clear guidelines, providing training and development opportunities, and establishing accountability mechanisms. It also necessitates a willingness to embrace feedback, to learn from mistakes, and to continuously adapt and improve.

The integration of spirituality and business is not a one-size-fits-all solution. The specific approach will vary depending on the nature of the organization, its culture, and the beliefs of its employees. However, the core principles remain consistent. By embracing these values, businesses can create a more ethical, sustainable, and ultimately, successful enterprise. This isn't merely about increasing profits; it's about creating a positive impact on the world and building a better future for all stakeholders. It's about recognizing that true success is measured not only by financial gains but also by the positive contribution made to society and the environment. This holistic approach to business is not simply a trend; it represents a fundamental shift in how we understand and define success in the 21st century and beyond. It's a paradigm shift that acknowledges the inherent value of all stakeholders and the interconnectedness of all systems, paving the way for a more sustainable, equitable, and fulfilling future for both business and humanity. The path forward requires courageous leadership, a willingness to question established norms, and a deep commitment to creating a more meaningful and purposeful way of doing business. The rewards – a more engaged workforce, stronger customer relationships, a positive impact on society, and ultimately, a more sustainable and profitable business – are worth the effort. This is the future of conscious capitalism, a model where profit and purpose walk hand-in-hand, creating a positive and enduring impact on the world.

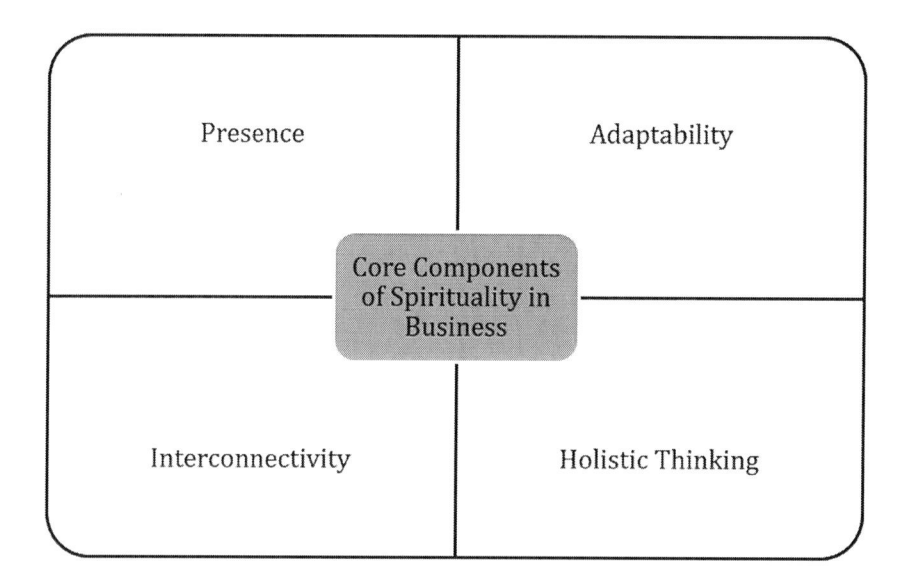

Presence	Adaptability
Core Components of Spirituality in Business	
Interconnectivity	Holistic Thinking

Reflection

2. Developing Your Spiritual Intelligence

Developing a robust spiritual intelligence is not about embracing a particular religion or dogma; rather, it's about cultivating an inner awareness and wisdom that informs all aspects of leadership. It's about accessing a deeper level of understanding, one that transcends the limitations of purely rational thought and allows for a more intuitive and ethical approach to decision-making. This involves developing *self-awareness, cultivating intuition, and fostering inner wisdom–* all essential components of conscious leadership.

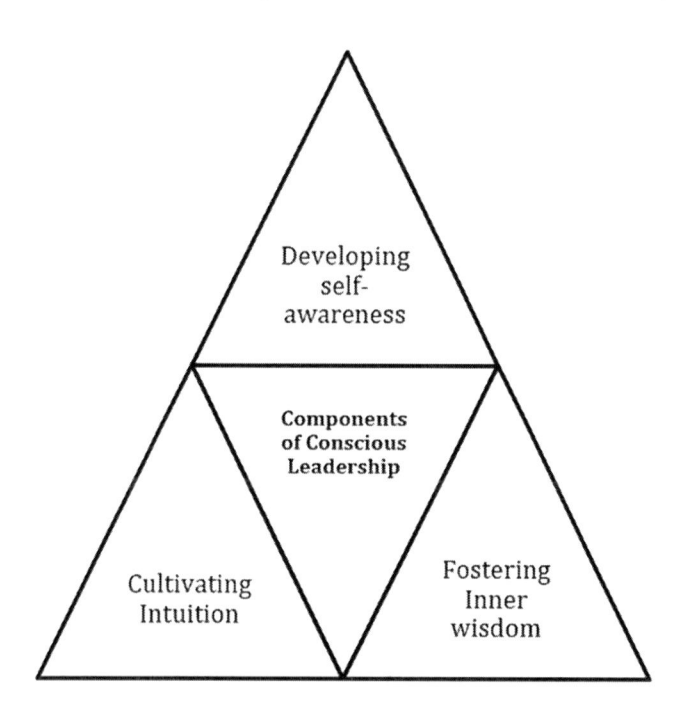

- Developing self-awareness
- **Components of Conscious Leadership**
- Cultivating Intuition
- Fostering Inner wisdom

Self-awareness, the cornerstone of spiritual intelligence, is the ability to understand one's own emotions, thoughts, and motivations. It's about recognizing the patterns of our behavior, identifying our strengths and weaknesses, and understanding how our actions impact others. This is not a passive process; it requires introspection, honest self- reflection, and a willingness to confront uncomfortable truths about us. Journaling can be a powerful tool for deepening self-awareness, providing a space to explore our thoughts and feelings without judgment. Regular journaling prompts can be crafted to focus on specific areas like identifying recurring emotional patterns, exploring limiting beliefs, and recognizing the impact of one's actions on others. Mindfulness practices, like meditation, can also significantly enhance self-awareness. By focusing on the present moment, without judgment, we become more attuned to our internal state, observing our thoughts and emotions as they arise, rather than being swept away by them.

The **Cultivation of Intuition**, often overlooked in traditional leadership models, is another critical aspect of developing spiritual intelligence. Intuition is that inner knowing, that gut feeling, that often guides us towards the right decision even when we lack complete information. It's a subtle form of intelligence, drawing upon both conscious and unconscious knowledge to provide insights that may not be immediately apparent through rational analysis alone. However, intuition is not merely a mystical ability; it's a skill that can be developed and refined through practice. This involves creating space for quiet contemplation, allowing for the emergence of inner wisdom. Practicing mindfulness and meditation creates that space, enabling a deeper connection to our inner voice and the intuitive guidance it offers. Regular practice of intuition-building exercises such as focusing on a problem and then deliberately letting go of conscious thought, allowing for an intuitive response to arise, can be highly effective. This involves trusting the subtle cues, the hunches, the quiet whispers of intuition, and acting on them with discernment.

Inner wisdom, the culmination of self-awareness and intuition, is the ability to access a deeper wellspring of knowledge and understanding. It's a synthesized blend of our experiences, our values, and our connection to something larger than ourselves. It provides a moral compass, guiding our actions towards ethical and sustainable outcomes. Inner wisdom is nurtured through reflection, introspection, and a commitment to ongoing personal growth. Learning to discern between intuition and impulsive reactions is a crucial aspect of developing this inner wisdom. It's about knowing when to trust your gut and when to seek more information. Reading widely on subjects relevant to leadership and conscious business practices help to expand our understanding and inform our intuition. Engaging in conversations with mentors and peers, seeking feedback and diverse perspectives, adds valuable layers to our own experience and strengthens our inner wisdom. Taking time for solitude, for quiet reflection, away from the demands of daily life, is essential to cultivating this deeper wisdom. This might involve regular retreats, silent meditation periods, or even simply carving out time each day for quiet contemplation.

The integration of spiritual intelligence into leadership practices transforms the very nature of decision-making. Instead of relying solely on logic and analysis, leaders tap into a wider range of knowledge, drawing upon their intuition, their self-awareness, and their inner wisdom to make more informed and ethical choices. This approach fosters a sense of purpose and meaning, inspiring both the leader and the team to strive for greater things. This holistic approach considers the impact of decisions not only on the bottom line, but also on employees, customers, and the wider community. Ethical considerations are not an afterthought, but an integral part of the decision-making process.

Meditation and mindfulness techniques are powerful tools for developing spiritual intelligence. Meditation cultivates a state of focused attention, quieting the mental chatter and enabling access to deeper levels of awareness. Regular meditation practice enhances self-awareness, allowing us to observe our thoughts and emotions without judgment, fostering greater emotional regulation and cultivating a sense of inner peace. Mindfulness, the practice of paying attention to the present moment without judgment, helps us to become more fully present in our interactions with others, enhancing empathy and compassion. Mindful leadership involves being fully present with our team, listening attentively, and responding with understanding and compassion. This mindful approach is far more effective in building strong relationships and fostering a sense of trust and collaboration.

Developing spiritual intelligence is not a destination, but an ongoing journey of self-discovery and growth. It's about consistently cultivating self-awareness, nurturing intuition, and accessing inner wisdom. It's about integrating these qualities into all aspects of leadership, creating a more ethical, compassionate, and sustainable approach to business. It requires consistent effort and self-reflection, a willingness to confront uncomfortable truths, and a commitment to ongoing personal and professional development. It's about embracing the journey, recognizing that the path to true leadership is a path of continual self-improvement, self-reflection, and a genuine commitment to personal growth.

The practical application of spiritual intelligence in leadership manifests in various ways. For instance, during challenging situations, a leader with developed spiritual intelligence might pause, engage in a brief mindfulness exercise, and access their intuition before reacting impulsively. This measured response allows for a more considered and ethical approach, minimizing the likelihood of regrettable decisions. In team dynamics, such a leader would prioritize open communication, active listening, and empathy, fostering a collaborative environment where every team member feels valued and heard. This creates a more harmonious and productive workplace where creativity flourishes and innovation thrive.

Further, in strategic planning, a spiritually intelligent leader would consider the long-term implications of decisions, not only in terms of profits but also in terms of environmental and social impact. This holistic approach demonstrates a commitment to sustainability and responsible business practices, building trust and loyalty among stakeholders.

This long-term perspective also allows for more resilient decision-making, navigating unforeseen circumstances with greater adaptability and grace. Spiritual intelligence isn't about ignoring the realities of the business world; instead, it's about approaching these challenges with a deeper level of wisdom, compassion, and ethical awareness.

The development of spiritual intelligence is an ongoing process, requiring consistent effort and dedication. It's a journey of self-discovery that requires a willingness to embrace vulnerability, acknowledge limitations, and cultivate inner peace. It necessitates incorporating practices like regular meditation, mindfulness exercises, and self-reflection into daily routines, not as mere add-ons but as fundamental aspects of personal and professional development. By consistently nurturing these practices, leaders can cultivate a deeper connection to their intuition, enhance their self-awareness, and tap into a wellspring of inner wisdom that guides them towards making ethically sound and sustainable decisions.

Ultimately, the integration of spiritual intelligence into leadership represents a shift towards a more holistic and human-centric approach to business. It's about moving beyond a purely transactional model of leadership towards one that embraces purpose, values, and ethical responsibility. This approach is not only personally fulfilling for the leader but also creates a more positive and fulfilling work environment for everyone involved, contributing to a more sustainable and just global economy. The conscious leader, grounded in spiritual intelligence, is not just a manager of resources but a steward of human potential and a guardian of ethical principles. This leadership model fosters a culture of collaboration, trust, and mutual respect, leading to increased productivity, enhanced employee engagement, and ultimately, a more meaningful and successful organization.

The journey of developing spiritual intelligence is a transformative one, leading to a more profound understanding of oneself and a deeper connection to the world around us. This, in turn, creates a ripple effect, positively influencing every facet of the organization and society as a whole.

Reflection

3. Holistic Decision Making and Systems Thinking

The traditional, reductionist way of making business decisions looks at each part—like finance, marketing, or operations—on its own and tries to improve them separately. But this narrow view overlooks how all these areas are deeply connected. In truth, a business is a complex system where every part influences the others, and focusing on one in isolation can lead to unintended consequences elsewhere.

A quantum approach necessitates a shift to a holistic viewpoint, acknowledging the intricate web of relationships between all aspects of the business and its environment. Holistic decision-making, informed by systems thinking, recognizes that every action has consequences that ripple outwards, affecting not only the immediate stakeholders but also the broader ecosystem. It's about understanding the intricate dance of cause and effect, recognizing that seemingly isolated decisions can have unforeseen and far-reaching impacts. This approach requires a shift from linear, cause-and-effect thinking to a more circular, interconnected understanding of reality. Instead of seeking optimal solutions for individual components, the focus shifts to optimizing the entire system as a whole. This necessitates a deep understanding of the relationships between different parts of the business and their environment. Systems thinking provides the conceptual framework for this holistic approach. It emphasizes the importance of understanding the whole before understanding the parts, recognizing that the properties of the whole are not simply the sum of its parts. Instead, emergent properties arise from the interactions and relationships between different components. For example, the overall performance of a business is not just the sum of the performance of its individual departments; it's also shaped by the interactions and synergies (or conflicts) between them.

Applying systems thinking to business decisions involves several key steps. First, it necessitates identifying all stakeholders involved, directly or indirectly, in the decision-making process. This goes beyond the usual suspects of shareholders, employees, and customers. It includes suppliers, distributors, communities, the environment, and even future generations. Stakeholder mapping, a powerful tool in systems thinking, can help visualize these complex relationships and assess the potential impact of decisions on each stakeholder group. A detailed stakeholder map can illuminate unforeseen consequences and help ensure that decisions are ethically sound and sustainable. For instance, a decision to outsource manufacturing to a lower-cost country might reduce production costs, benefiting shareholders in the short term. However, the stakeholder map would highlight potential negative impacts on workers in the original location, the environment in the new location, and the company's brand reputation.

Scenario planning is another crucial tool within a holistic decision-making framework. Instead of focusing on a single, most likely future, scenario planning involves developing multiple alternative future scenarios, each based on different assumptions about key drivers and uncertainties. This allows for a more robust and adaptable response to unexpected events. For instance, a company might develop scenarios based on different levels of economic growth, regulatory changes, or technological advancements. By anticipating a range of possibilities, the organization can develop contingency plans and make more informed decisions that are less vulnerable to unforeseen circumstances.

The use of feedback loops is central to effective systems thinking. A feedback loop is a cyclical process where the output of a system influences its subsequent input, creating a dynamic and ever-evolving system. Understanding these loops is crucial for predicting the long-term consequences of decisions and ensuring that the system remains stable and sustainable. For example, a company that implements a new marketing campaign might observe increased sales (positive feedback loop), but this could lead to increased demand for resources, potentially creating supply chain bottlenecks and ultimately limiting growth. Understanding this feedback loop allows the company to proactively adjust its marketing strategy and resource allocation to ensure sustainable growth.

The quantum principle of entanglement further underscores the interconnectedness inherent in systems thinking. Entanglement suggests that seemingly disparate components of a system are intrinsically linked, meaning that changes in one part of the system inevitably affect other parts. This highlights the crucial importance of holistic decision-making, as isolated actions can have unintended and far-reaching consequences. Understanding these entangled relationships helps businesses to anticipate and manage these potential ripple effects.

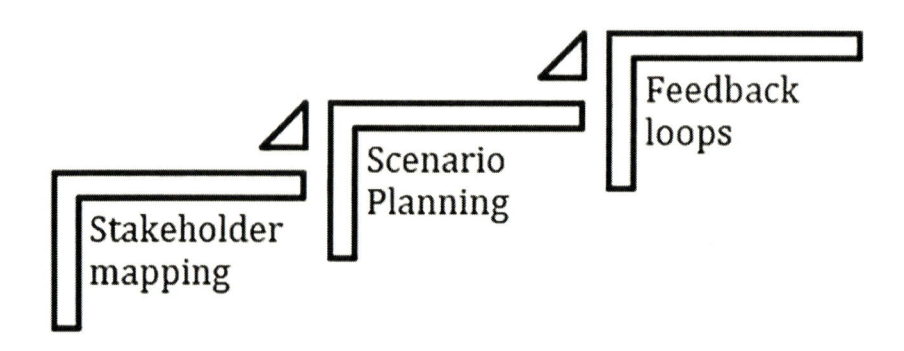

System Thinking Steps

- Stakeholder mapping
- Scenario Planning
- Feedback loops

Moving beyond traditional metrics, a quantum business embraces a broader set of indicators to measure success. While financial performance remains important, a holistic view incorporates social, environmental, and ethical measures. The triple bottom line – profit, people, and planet–provides a framework for evaluating the overall impact of business decisions. Consider a company striving for sustainable agriculture. While profit is a key driver, measuring the positive impact on soil health, biodiversity, and farmer livelihoods provides a more complete picture of success than financial metrics alone. This holistic approach goes beyond simply satisfying minimum standards; it embraces a commitment to continual improvement and proactively seeks to exceed expectations.

A key aspect of holistic decision-making is the cultivation of mindfulness and intuition. While data and analysis are crucial, a quantum approach values the insights gained through mindful reflection and intuitive awareness. This enables leaders to tap into a deeper understanding of the system and make more informed and responsible choices.

This doesn't imply disregarding data; rather, it suggests integrating data-driven analysis with intuitive insights to achieve a more comprehensive understanding. For example, a leader might analyze sales data to identify trends but also consult with employees on the ground to gain a deeper understanding of customer preferences and market dynamics.

Implementing holistic decision-making and systems thinking requires a fundamental shift in organizational culture. It necessitates a move away from a siloed approach to one of collaboration and shared understanding. This involves fostering open communication, transparency, and a willingness to embrace complexity and uncertainty. Leadership plays a critical role in driving this transformation, fostering a culture that values learning, adaptation, and a commitment to long-term sustainability. This shift requires investment in training and development to equip employees with the necessary systems thinking skills and empower them to contribute to holistic decision-making.

In conclusion, embracing holistic decision-making and systems thinking is not merely a philosophical exercise; it's a practical necessity for navigating the complexities of the modern business environment. By understanding the interconnectedness of all aspects of the business and its environment, leaders can make more informed, responsible, and sustainable decisions that contribute to the long-term success and flourishing of both the business and the wider world. This approach, deeply rooted in quantum principles, acknowledges the inherent interconnectedness of reality and empowers businesses to become integral parts of a thriving and sustainable ecosystem. The ripple effect of conscious, holistic decision-making extends far beyond the immediate business sphere, creating positive change within communities, ecosystems, and the global economy. It is a journey of continuous learning, adaptation, and a commitment to evolving alongside the complex adaptive systems in which businesses operate.

Reflection

4. Harnessing Intuition in Decision Making

Harnessing intuition in decision-making requires a nuanced understanding of its nature and a conscious effort to cultivate it. It's not about abandoning logic or data-driven analysis; instead, it's about integrating intuition as a complementary and powerful tool within the decision-making process. This subconscious processing is informed by years of accumulated experience, both personal and professional, shaping the intuitive insights we receive.

Consider a seasoned entrepreneur facing a critical business decision, such as launching a new product line or entering a new market. They might meticulously analyze market research, financial projections, and competitor strategies, utilizing their rational mind to evaluate the risks and rewards. However, simultaneously, their intuition – shaped by years of business experience and an understanding of market trends – might whisper a sense of unease, or conversely, a powerful sense of confidence about a particular path. This intuitive feeling, while not quantifiable in the same way as market data, often proves remarkably accurate. Ignoring this valuable input would be a significant oversight.

The key lies in learning to discern between true intuition and mere emotional reactivity. Impulsive reactions, often driven by fear or anxiety, are not the same as intuitive insights.

Intuition arises from a calm and centered state of mind, a space where clarity and discernment are more readily available. Cultivating this state of mind through practices like mindfulness meditation is crucial for accessing and interpreting intuitive guidance effectively. The more we practice mindfulness, the sharper our ability to differentiate between fleeting emotions and the deeper, more considered wisdom that arises from our intuition.

One practical strategy for harnessing intuition is **to create dedicated time for quiet reflection before making significant decisions**. This might involve a brief period of mindful meditation, a walk in nature, or simply sitting quietly with the problem at hand. During this time, actively resist the urge to analyze or overthink; instead, focus on feeling into the situation. Pay attention to the subtle physical sensations in your body – a tightening in the chest, a lightness in the heart– that often accompany intuitive insights. These physical cues can be incredibly valuable indicators, signaling whether a particular course of action feels right or wrong, aligned or misaligned with your deeper sense of purpose.

Another effective technique is **to utilize intuition-building exercises**. For example, when facing a complex problem, try writing down all the facts and figures that you have, consciously trying to make sense of them. Once you feel you've exhausted the rational approach, let go of the intellectual effort, and simply focus on the problem itself. Allow your mind to wander freely, without judgment. Often, an intuitive answer will emerge – a fresh perspective, a novel approach, or a profound insight that wasn't accessible through rational analysis alone. It's important to remember that intuition is not a magic bullet. It doesn't provide all the answers instantly, nor does it replace the need for thorough research and planning. Rather, it acts as a compass, guiding us towards the most appropriate direction. It provides a sense of alignment, helping us determine whether a particular course of action resonates with our values, our vision, and our sense of purpose.

Integrating intuition with rational analysis allows for a more holistic approach, leading to more balanced and insightful decisions. The process of integrating intuition into decision-making also involves **cultivating trust in one's own inner wisdom**. This requires overcoming self-doubt and the tendency to prioritize external validation over internal guidance. It's a matter of actively choosing to listen to that quiet inner voice, even when it contradicts the conventional wisdom or the opinions of others. Building this trust necessitates consistent practice and a willingness to acknowledge and learn from both successes and failures. Over time, as you learn to trust your intuition more consistently, your confidence in your decision-making abilities will naturally increase.

Furthermore, **cultivating a strong connection to one's values** is essential for effectively harnessing intuition. Our values serve as a filter, guiding our intuitive insights towards choices that align with our deeper sense of purpose and meaning. When our intuition resonates with our values, we have a stronger sense of conviction and commitment to the decisions we make, leading to greater resilience and effectiveness in the face of challenges. Conversely, when our intuition points towards a course of action that conflicts with our values, it's a signal to pause, reconsider, and potentially explore alternative options.

Another important aspect is **the integration of diverse perspectives**. While intuition provides a valuable inner compass, it's essential to avoid becoming insular or overly reliant on one's own perspective. Seeking diverse perspectives, actively listening to the opinions and experiences of others, enhances our understanding of the situation at hand and can enrich our intuitive insights. Engaging in constructive dialogue with trusted advisors, colleagues, or mentors can offer valuable insights that complement and refine our intuitive guidance.

Developing a strong intuition is also closely related to emotional intelligence. The ability to understand and manage one's own emotions, as well as the emotions of others, is crucial for discerning true intuition and emotional reactivity. A leader with high emotional intelligence is better equipped to recognize the subtle emotional cues that accompany intuitive insights, distinguishing them from impulsive reactions driven by fear or anxiety.

Finally, remember that harnessing intuition is an ongoing process, not a destination. It requires continuous self- reflection, the willingness to learn from mistakes, and a commitment to nurture the qualities of self-awareness, mindfulness, and inner wisdom. The more we practice these qualities, the stronger our intuition becomes, and the more effectively we can integrate it into our decision-making processes. Ultimately, the integration of intuition into leadership and decision-making allow for a more holistic and ethically aligned approach, fostering greater creativity, resilience, and a deeper sense of purpose. It is a path towards more balanced, insightful, and ultimately more successful outcomes. By combining rational analysis with intuitive guidance, leaders can navigate the complexities of the business world with greater wisdom, compassion, and effectiveness. This integrated approach represents a paradigm shift in leadership, moving beyond purely rational models to embrace a more holistic and human-centered approach that aligns with the deeper needs and aspirations of both individuals and organizations.

Reflection

5. Cultivating Mindfulness and Presence

Mindfulness, often misunderstood as a mere relaxation technique, is in reality a powerful tool for cultivating presence and enhancing leadership capabilities. It's about cultivating a heightened awareness of the present moment, without judgment. In the fast-paced world of business, where constant multitasking and information overload are the norm, mindfulness acts as an anchor, grounding us in the here and now and allowing us to respond to challenges with greater clarity and composure. This heightened awareness allows for a more nuanced understanding of our own emotions and the emotions of others, which is crucial for effective leadership.

The benefits of mindfulness practices extend far beyond stress reduction. While reducing stress is undoubtedly a significant advantage—stress impairs decision-making, fosters reactivity, and diminishes creativity—the true power of mindfulness lies in its ability to sharpen our focus, enhance our emotional intelligence, and foster a deeper connection with our intuition. When we're present, we're better able to receive and interpret the subtle cues that our intuition provides. We're less likely to be swayed by impulsive reactions or biases and more likely to make decisions that are aligned with our values and our long-term goals.

Consider a leader facing a conflict between team members. A leader operating from a place of reactivity might escalate the conflict, potentially causing further damage to team morale and productivity. However, a mindful leader, by cultivating presence, can observe the situation without judgment, recognizing the emotions involved—both their own and those of the team members. This allows for a more compassionate and effective response, potentially de-escalating the conflict and fostering a more collaborative environment. This ability to understand and manage emotions—both one's own and those of others—is the very essence of emotional intelligence, a critical skill for any leader.

Mindfulness practices are not esoteric or complex; they are readily accessible to anyone willing to dedicate time and effort. One of the most widely practiced mindfulness techniques is **meditation**. Meditation doesn't require a secluded monastery or years of rigorous training; it simply involves sitting quietly, focusing on the breath, and observing the thoughts and sensations that arise without judgment. Even just five to ten minutes of daily meditation can have a profound impact on one's ability to focus, manage stress, and enhance emotional intelligence. There are numerous guided meditations available online and through apps, making it easy to integrate this practice into one's daily routine.

Deep breathing exercises are another readily accessible mindfulness technique. Consciously slowing and deepening our breath can instantly calm the nervous system, reducing stress and promoting a sense of calmness and clarity. Deep breathing techniques can be integrated into one's daily life, used as needed to manage stressful situations or simply as a regular practice to cultivate presence. A simple technique involves inhaling deeply through the nose, holding the breath for a few seconds, and then exhaling slowly through the mouth. Repeating this process several times can significantly reduce anxiety and promote a state of calmness.

Body scans are yet another powerful technique for cultivating mindfulness. A body scan involves systematically bringing attention to different parts of the body, noticing sensations without judgment. This practice can enhance body awareness, helping us to recognize the physical cues that often accompany our emotions and intuition. For instance, a tightening in the chest might signal anxiety, while a lightness in the heart might indicate joy or confidence. Recognizing these physical cues allows for a more nuanced understanding of our inner world. Regular body scans can also improve our self-awareness, leading to greater emotional intelligence.

Mindful walking is a deceptively simple yet profoundly effective way to cultivate presence. Instead of rushing from one task to the next, consciously slow down and pay attention to the sensations of walking—the feeling of the ground beneath your feet, the rhythm of your breath, the movement of your body. This practice helps to ground us in the present moment, reducing the tendency to dwell on past events or worry about the future. It's a practice easily integrated into one's daily routine, requiring no special equipment or location. It can be as simple as taking a mindful walk during a lunch break or a mindful stroll before beginning the workday.

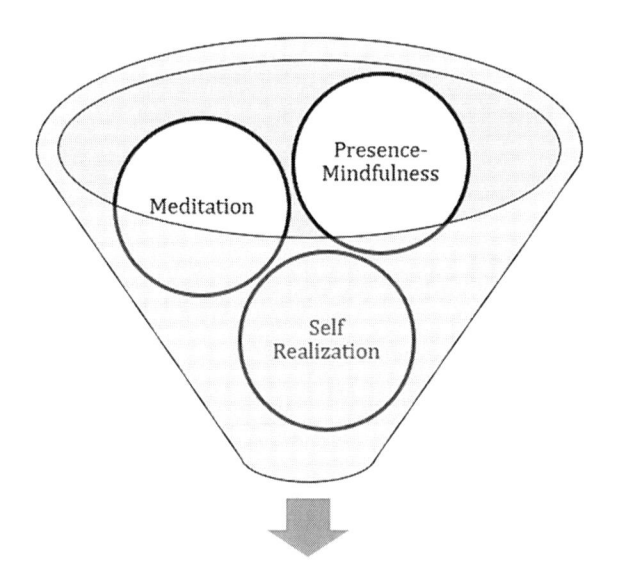

Spiritual Intelligence

Beyond formal practices like meditation and deep breathing, mindfulness can be woven into the fabric of our daily lives. Paying attention to the simple acts of eating, drinking, or listening can become a mindfulness practice. Savoring the taste of food, noticing the temperature of the water, and truly listening to what another person is saying, without interrupting or planning our response, all contribute to a greater sense of presence. This mindful engagement with daily life enhances our awareness and cultivates a more appreciative attitude toward our surroundings.

Furthermore, integrating mindfulness into leadership requires a conscious commitment to self-reflection. Regular self-reflection allows leaders to examine their thoughts, feelings, and behaviors without judgment. This self-awareness is crucial for recognizing our own biases and blind spots, enabling us to lead with greater empathy and understanding. Journaling is a valuable tool for self-reflection. Writing down our thoughts and feelings can help us to process experiences, identify patterns, and gain insights into our own behavior.

Leading with presence also entails cultivating empathy and active listening. Active listening involves fully focusing on the speaker, without interrupting or formulating a response. It's about truly hearing what the other person is saying, both verbally and nonverbally. By fully engaging with the speaker, leaders foster deeper connections, build trust, and gain a richer understanding of diverse perspectives.

In the context of business decisions, mindfulness offers a crucial advantage. By cultivating presence, leaders can avoid the trap of making hasty decisions based on incomplete information or emotional reactivity. Instead, they can take the time to gather information, consider different perspectives, and access their intuition, leading to more informed and balanced decisions. The ability to remain calm and centered under pressure is invaluable in high-stakes situations.

The integration of mindfulness into leadership is not a one-time event but rather a continuous process of learning and refinement. It demands consistent effort, self-compassion, and a willingness to embrace mistakes as learning opportunities. The journey of cultivating mindfulness is a personal one, and the techniques that work for one person may not work for another. Experimentation and self-discovery are crucial to finding the practices that resonate most deeply.

However, the rewards of cultivating mindfulness far outweigh the effort required. A mindful leader is better equipped to navigate the complexities of the business world, fostering a more positive and productive work environment, making more balanced and informed decisions, and ultimately achieving greater success—both personally and professionally. This conscious leadership style fosters a culture of well-being, collaboration, and ethical decision-making, ultimately benefiting both the organization and its stakeholders. It reflects a shift towards a more human-centered approach to leadership, recognizing the importance of emotional intelligence, self-awareness, and compassion in fostering genuine success and lasting impact. In a world increasingly dominated by technology and rapid change, the ability to remain present, grounded, and compassionate becomes a key differentiator, a cornerstone of effective and ethically aligned leadership.

Reflection

6. Ethical Frameworks for Decision Making

Building upon the foundation of mindfulness and its role in enhancing leadership, we now turn our attention to the crucial aspect of ethical decision-making. In the complex landscape of business, where profits often clash with values, a robust ethical framework is not merely a desirable trait but a necessity for sustainable success and genuine leadership. The absence of a clear ethical compass can lead to compromised integrity, damaged reputations, and ultimately, the erosion of trust, the very cornerstone of any successful enterprise.

This section explores several prominent ethical frameworks that can serve as guiding principles for navigating the ethical dilemmas inherent in leadership and business decisions. Understanding these frameworks provides leaders with a structured approach to evaluating choices, ensuring decisions align with their personal values and contribute to a more responsible and sustainable business model.

One of the most widely discussed ethical frameworks is **utilitarianism**. At its core, utilitarianism focuses on maximizing overall happiness and minimizing harm.

Decisions are judged based on their consequences, with the most ethical choice being the one that produces the greatest good for the greatest number of people. In a business context, a utilitarian approach might involve choosing the course of action that maximizes shareholder value while minimizing negative impacts on employees, customers, and the environment. However, the application of utilitarianism can be complex. Determining the "greatest good" often requires careful consideration of various stakeholders and potential consequences, which can be challenging in situations with conflicting interests. For example, a company might face a decision between investing in a new technology that increases efficiency and profitability but leads to job losses, or maintaining the status quo, preserving jobs but limiting potential growth. A utilitarian approach requires a rigorous cost-benefit analysis, carefully weighing the potential positive and negative outcomes for all stakeholders. Moreover, predicting the long-term consequences of any decision is often difficult, rendering the utilitarian calculation inherently uncertain.

In contrast to utilitarianism's focus on consequences, **deontology** emphasizes the inherent rightness or wrongness of actions themselves, regardless of their outcomes.

Deontological frameworks, often associated with the philosophy of Immanuel Kant, emphasize moral duties and principles, such as honesty, fairness, and respect for individuals. A deontological approach to business decisions prioritizes adherence to ethical rules and principles, even if doing so might lead to less desirable outcomes. For example, a company might choose not to engage in a potentially lucrative deal if it involves compromising its commitment to environmental sustainability or fair labor practices. While deontology provides a clear and consistent ethical framework, its rigidity can sometimes lead to conflicts. Situations might arise where adhering to one ethical principle clashes with another, creating difficult choices.

Imagine a scenario where a company faces a legal requirement that conflicts with its commitment to transparent communication with its stakeholders. Choosing between legal compliance and ethical transparency requires careful consideration and a nuanced understanding of the relevant principles involved.

Virtue ethics offers a different perspective, focusing on the character of the moral agent rather than the consequences of actions or adherence to rules. It emphasizes cultivating moral virtues, such as honesty, integrity, compassion, and courage, which then guide ethical decision-making. Virtue ethics suggests that individuals who cultivate these virtues are more likely to make ethical choices consistently, regardless of the specific situation. In a business context, this means fostering a culture that values ethical behavior, providing training and support for employees to develop moral virtues, and holding leaders accountable for their actions. This approach focuses on developing the moral character of individuals within the organization, empowering them to make ethical choices independently and fostering a strong ethical culture. The challenge with virtue ethics lies in defining and operationalizing these virtues within a specific business context. What constitutes "honesty" or "integrity" might vary depending on cultural norms and industry practices. Moreover, judging an individual's character based on a single decision can be misleading; a person's virtue is revealed through consistent patterns of behavior over time.

Integrating these ethical frameworks into a conscious leadership approach requires a nuanced understanding of their strengths and limitations. It's not about rigidly adhering to a single framework but rather using them as complementary tools for navigating ethical dilemmas. A leader might begin by considering the potential consequences of different options through a utilitarian lens, then assess the ethical implications of each choice based on deontological principles, and finally evaluate whether the decision aligns with their own moral character and the virtues they aspire to embody. This multi-faceted approach ensures a more comprehensive and responsible decision-making process.

Furthermore, ethical decision-making is not a solitary exercise; it demands collaboration and transparency.

Engaging stakeholders in the process, including employees, customers, suppliers, and community members, ensures that diverse perspectives are considered and that decisions reflect a shared understanding of ethical responsibilities. Open communication and a culture of trust are crucial for fostering ethical behavior and building a more responsible business. This inclusive approach involves actively seeking feedback, addressing concerns, and demonstrating a commitment to transparency and accountability.

Beyond these frameworks, it's vital to consider the broader context of corporate social responsibility (CSR). CSR extends beyond simply complying with legal requirements and encompasses a company's commitment to acting ethically and sustainably, contributing to the well-being of society and the environment. Integrating CSR into business strategy requires a holistic approach, considering not only the financial implications of decisions but also their social and environmental impact. This might involve investing in sustainable practices, supporting community initiatives, or promoting ethical sourcing. A conscious business leader understands that long-term success is inextricably linked to ethical conduct and social responsibility.

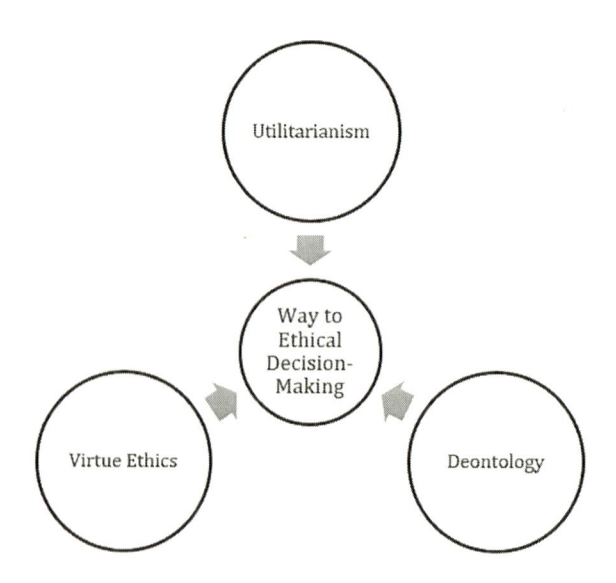

```
        Utilitarianism
              ↓
        Way to
        Ethical
       Decision-
        Making
       ↗        ↖
Virtue Ethics   Deontology
```

In conclusion, leading with intuition and wisdom necessitates a firm grasp of ethical frameworks. While utilitarianism, deontology, and virtue ethics each offer unique perspectives, their combined application provides a powerful toolset for navigating complex ethical dilemmas. By integrating these frameworks, embracing corporate social responsibility, and fostering a culture of collaboration and transparency, conscious leaders can make responsible choices that contribute to sustainable business success, a positive impact on society, and ultimately, a more meaningful and fulfilling leadership journey. The path towards ethical leadership is not a destination but a continuous journey of learning, reflection, and a steadfast commitment to integrity. It requires continuous learning, self-reflection, and a willingness to adapt and evolve as ethical challenges emerge. This ongoing process of ethical development is crucial for leaders who aspire to build thriving, responsible organizations and to leave a lasting positive impact on the world. The ultimate goal is to create businesses that not only generate profits but also contribute to a more just, equitable, and sustainable future for all stakeholders.

Reflection

7. The Power of Forgiveness and Letting Go

The journey of conscious leadership is not solely defined by strategic planning and ethical frameworks; it's deeply intertwined with the capacity for emotional intelligence and spiritual maturity. A crucial element often overlooked in the pursuit of business success is the power of forgiveness and the art of letting go. These aren't merely sentimental notions; they are potent catalysts for personal growth and transformative leadership. Holding onto resentment, anger, and past hurts creates internal friction, hindering clear decision-making, and poisoning relationships—all vital components of a thriving organization.

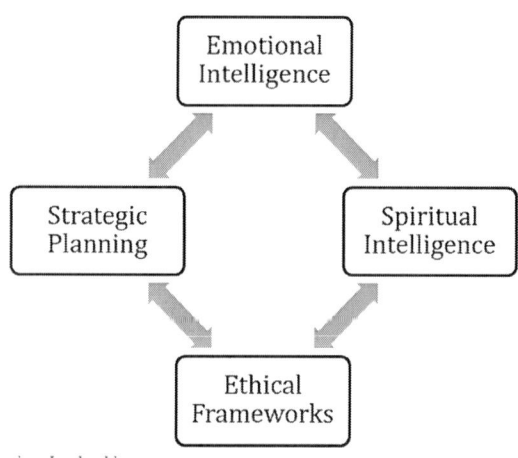

Journey of Conscious Leadership

Forgiveness, in the context of leadership, encompasses far more than simply excusing wrongdoing. It's an active process of releasing the emotional grip of past transgressions, both those inflicted upon us and those we have committed. When we harbor resentment towards employees, colleagues, competitors, or even customers, we essentially allow negativity to cloud our judgment and limit our potential for empathy and understanding. This negativity manifests in various ways—from subtle biases in decision-making to overt expressions of hostility, creating a toxic work environment and hindering collaborative efforts.

Consider the scenario of a team member who consistently misses deadlines, causing setbacks for the entire project. The initial reaction might be anger and frustration. However, a conscious leader would recognize that this behavior likely stems from underlying issues, perhaps a lack of skills, personal challenges, or even systemic problems within the organization. Instead of dwelling on the negative impact of the missed deadlines, a leader who embraces forgiveness would seek to understand the root cause, providing support and guidance to help the team members improve their performance. This approach fosters trust, encourages self-improvement, and strengthens the overall team dynamic. It's about moving beyond blame and towards a solution-oriented approach.

Furthermore, forgiveness extends to the self. Leaders are not immune to making mistakes. We all make errors in judgment, miscalculations, and sometimes, even unethical choices. The capacity to forgive oneself is crucial for personal growth and for creating a culture of learning within the organization. When we hold ourselves to impossibly high standards, beating ourselves up over past failures, we create a cycle of self-criticism that hinders our ability to move forward and learn from our experiences. Forgiving ourselves allows us to acknowledge our mistakes without dwelling on them, transforming them into valuable learning opportunities. It also allows us to model vulnerability and authenticity, creating a more supportive and compassionate work environment.

Letting go complements forgiveness, representing the deliberate act of releasing negative emotions and thoughts that no longer serve us. This is especially important in the fast-paced, often stressful environment of the business world. It requires conscious effort and practice, recognizing that clinging to negative emotions consumes energy and hinders our ability to focus on present opportunities and challenges. Letting go might involve setting boundaries, terminating unproductive relationships, or relinquishing control over aspects beyond our influence.

Imagine a scenario where a promising business venture fails despite rigorous planning and execution. The leader might experience significant disappointment, even self-doubt. However, a conscious leader who practices letting go would acknowledge the disappointment without allowing it to consume them. They would analyze the factors contributing to the failure, extract valuable lessons, and move on to new opportunities, applying the hard-won wisdom gained from the experience. This ability to detach from the outcome and focus on learning from setbacks is paramount for resilience and long-term success.

This practice of letting go extends beyond personal experiences to encompass organizational changes and setbacks. The business world is inherently dynamic, subject to market fluctuations, technological disruptions, and unforeseen challenges. Clinging to outdated strategies or resisting change will hinder adaptation and growth. A conscious leader embraces change, recognizing that letting go of old paradigms is crucial for innovation and long-term sustainability. This might involve restructuring departments, adopting new technologies, or even re-evaluating the company's core mission in response to evolving market demands.

The integration of forgiveness and letting go requires intentional practice. Mindfulness meditation, journaling, and engaging in self-reflection are valuable tools that can help leaders cultivate these crucial qualities. Mindfulness, in particular, allows us to observe our thoughts and emotions without judgment, creating space to recognize and release negative patterns. Journaling helps us process our emotions, clarifying our thoughts and facilitating self-awareness. Regular self-reflection encourages self-compassion, providing opportunities to forgive ourselves and others. Furthermore, creating a culture of forgiveness and letting go within the organization is paramount. This requires fostering an environment of open communication, empathy, and mutual respect. Leaders must model these behaviors, creating space for employees to share their experiences, concerns, and even mistakes without fear of judgment. This creates a safe and supportive environment where individuals feel empowered to learn, grow, and contribute their best to the organization.

The benefits of incorporating forgiveness and letting go into leadership practices are manifold. It fosters healthier relationships, improved communication, increased collaboration, greater creativity, enhanced resilience, and ultimately, increased levels of both individual and organizational success. These are not merely abstract concepts; they are practical tools for cultivating a more compassionate, productive, and fulfilling workplace. The practice of forgiveness isn't a sign of weakness, but a testament to strength and maturity. It takes courage to confront past hurts, acknowledge our own imperfections, and release the burden of resentment. But in doing so, we free ourselves from the shackles of the past, allowing us to step into a future characterized by greater clarity, compassion, and a deeper understanding of ourselves and those around us. This profound shift in perspective fundamentally alters the leadership experience, transforming the business journey from a relentless pursuit of profit to a path of personal growth, ethical conduct, and collective well-being. It's about creating an organization where forgiveness is not just a policy, but a guiding principle, woven into the very fabric of the company culture. This creates an environment where mistakes are viewed as learning opportunities, and where employees feel valued, respected, and supported in their journey of professional growth.

The ultimate goal is to cultivate a business environment that mirrors the qualities we strive for in our personal lives—an environment characterized by compassion, understanding, and a shared commitment to growth and well-being. This is not simply about improving the bottom line; it's about building a thriving, ethical, and deeply human organization that makes a positive impact on the world. By embracing the power of forgiveness and the art of letting go, conscious leaders can create a legacy that extends far beyond the balance sheet, fostering a legacy of genuine connection, meaningful growth, and lasting positive change. This intentional shift in perspective not only benefits the individual leader but also shapes the culture of the entire organization, creating a more harmonious and productive work environment. This holistic approach to leadership allows for a more sustainable and successful future for both the business and the individuals within it. It's a testament to the power of mindful leadership and its transformative potential.

Reflection

Chapter 6: Conscious Capitalism in Action

		Empowering employees through purpose	Building ethical supply chains and partnerships	Transparency & Accountability in Operations
Measuring Impact beyond Bottom Line	Creating a values based culture	Defining your company's higher purpose		

Conscious Capitalism in Action

1. Measuring Impact Beyond the Bottom Line

Moving beyond the purely financial metrics of success, a truly conscious business recognizes the interconnectedness of its actions and their impact on all stakeholders–employees, customers, communities, and the environment. Profit, while essential for sustainability, is only one piece of the puzzle. A comprehensive understanding of impact necessitates a broader perspective, encompassing social and environmental considerations alongside the bottom line. This holistic approach requires the development and implementation of robust measurement systems that capture the multifaceted nature of a conscious business' contribution.

Traditional business models primarily focus on shareholder value, often neglecting the wider ecosystem in which they operate. However, a growing body of evidence demonstrates a strong correlation between corporate social responsibility (CSR) and long-term financial performance. Companies that prioritize ethical practices, environmental sustainability, and employee well-being often experience increased brand loyalty, enhanced reputation, improved employee engagement, and ultimately, greater profitability. This shift in perspective necessitates a corresponding shift in how we measure success.

Measuring the social and environmental impact of a business requires a move beyond simplistic, quantitative metrics. While financial indicators like revenue, profit margins, and return on investment (ROI) remain important, they offer an incomplete picture. We need to incorporate qualitative data that captures the intangible yet significant aspects of a business's influence. This includes factors like employee satisfaction, customer loyalty, community engagement, and environmental footprint.

One crucial area is employee well-being. A conscious business understands that its employees are its most valuable asset. Therefore, measuring employee satisfaction, engagement, and retention becomes paramount. This can be achieved through various methods, including regular employee surveys, anonymous feedback mechanisms, and 360-degree performance reviews. Analyzing this data allows businesses to identify areas for improvement, such as addressing workplace stress, enhancing work-life balance, or improving communication channels. High employee retention, coupled with positive employee feedback, directly correlates with increased productivity, reduced recruitment costs, and improved organizational culture.

Furthermore, understanding the social impact of a business extends beyond its immediate workforce. A conscious organization assesses its influence on the surrounding community. This may involve measuring local employment opportunities created, charitable contributions made, and community engagement initiatives undertaken. For example, a company might track the number of local residents employed, the amount invested in local infrastructure projects, or the participation rate in community volunteering programs. These data points provide valuable insights into a business's contribution to the social fabric of its community.

Environmental sustainability is another critical aspect to be measured. A conscious business strives to minimize its environmental footprint, taking responsibility for its impact on the planet. Metrics in this area can include carbon emissions, water consumption, waste generation, and energy efficiency. Utilizing tools like lifecycle assessments (LCAs) can help companies measure the environmental impact of their products and services from cradle to grave. By tracking these metrics, businesses can identify areas for improvement and implement strategies to reduce their environmental impact, aligning their operations with sustainability goals. This commitment to environmental stewardship not only reduces the company's environmental footprint but can also enhance brand image, attract environmentally conscious consumers, and potentially reduce operating costs.

Integrating these various metrics into a cohesive framework is crucial for effective measurement. Several frameworks exist, such as the Global Reporting Initiative (GRI) Standards, the Sustainability Accounting Standards Board (SASB) standards, and the United Nations Sustainable Development Goals (SDGs). These frameworks provide standardized guidelines for reporting on environmental, social, and governance (ESG) performance, allowing for greater transparency and comparability across different businesses. Adopting such a framework allows a business to establish a structured approach to measuring its holistic impact, ensuring consistent reporting and tracking of progress over time.

Beyond established frameworks, a company might create a customized impact measurement system tailored to its specific context and priorities. This approach allows for a deep dive into those aspects most relevant to the business's mission and values. However, it is vital that any customized system adheres to principles of transparency, objectivity, and reliability. Regular audits and independent verification can ensure the credibility and trustworthiness of the data collected. The choice of metrics and the methodology used should be clearly defined and documented to allow for consistent monitoring and evaluation of progress. The data gathered through these various measurement systems shouldn't simply be archived. It needs to be actively utilized to inform strategic decision-making and guide ongoing improvement. Regular review and analysis of the data allows businesses to pinpoint areas of strength and weakness, enabling the implementation of targeted interventions to maximize positive impact and mitigate negative consequences. This continuous improvement process is fundamental to the evolution of a truly conscious business. Regular reporting, both internally and externally, allows stakeholders to see the company's commitment and track its progress towards its stated goals. Transparency fosters trust and accountability, building stronger relationships with all stakeholders.

Measuring impact is not just about accumulating data; it's about using that data to create a virtuous cycle of improvement. The process of measuring, analyzing, and acting on the information gleaned offers valuable insights that lead to enhanced operational efficiency, increased employee engagement, stronger community ties, and a reduced environmental footprint. It strengthens the organization's resilience and adaptability in the face of evolving societal and environmental challenges. Furthermore, showcasing this holistic approach to impact measurement can enhance a business's reputation, attract investors who value sustainability, and ultimately, contribute to long-term financial success.

In conclusion, measuring impact in a conscious business requires a paradigm shift from a narrow focus on financial performance to a broader, more holistic perspective. By integrating social and environmental considerations into the measurement framework, businesses can gain a more complete understanding of their influence on the world.

Using a variety of metrics, from employee satisfaction to environmental impact, and adopting robust reporting frameworks, businesses can build a sustainable future that benefits all stakeholders. The continuous process of measurement, analysis, and improvement reinforces a commitment to conscious business practices and underscores the organization's commitment to a more just and sustainable world. This commitment not only enhances brand reputation but also contributes to the long-term viability and success of the organization, solidifying its position as a leader in conscious business practices.

"The true measure of a conscious business's success lies not just in its profits, but in the positive impact it creates on the world."

Reflection

2. Defining Your Company's Higher Purpose

Defining a company's higher purpose transcends the simplistic pursuit of profit maximization. It's about articulating a compelling narrative that resonates not only with employees and investors but also with customers and the wider community. This higher purpose serves as North Star, guiding strategic decisions, shaping organizational culture, and inspiring action. It's the bedrock upon which a truly conscious organization is built. It answers the fundamental question: "Why does our company exist beyond making money?" The answer must be profound, authentic, and deeply embedded in the organization's values.

This process of defining a higher purpose begins with introspection. It requires a deep dive into the company's history, examining its origins, its evolution, and the motivations of its founders. What were the initial driving forces behind its creation? What problems were they trying to solve? What unmet needs were they addressing? Understanding this genesis provides a foundation for crafting a purpose statement that resonates with the organization's core identity.

Next, the organization needs to identify its core values. These are the guiding principles that inform all aspects of the business, from employee interactions to product development and marketing strategies. These values should be more than just aspirational statements; they should be actively lived and embodied by every member of the organization. A conscious business actively cultivates a culture where these values are not just words on a wall, but the very fabric of daily operations. This requires open communication, feedback mechanisms, and ongoing reinforcement of the values through leadership behavior and organizational practices.

Once the core values are defined, the organization can then articulate its mission statement. This statement succinctly describes the organization's purpose and how it intends to achieve it. A powerful mission statement is concise, memorable, and inspiring, clearly communicating the organization's contribution to the world. It should answer the question: "What do we do, and why does it matter?" A strong mission statement transcends mere product or service descriptions; it connects the organization's activities to a larger, more meaningful purpose.

The vision statement then paints a picture of the desired future state. It's a long-term aspiration, a compelling image of what the organization hopes to achieve in the years to come. This vision provides a sense of direction and purpose, motivating employees to work towards a shared goal. A truly conscious vision statement goes beyond financial targets; it envisions a positive impact on society, the environment, or a specific community. It articulates the organization's contribution to a better world.

Crucially, the higher purpose must be authentic. It can't be a mere marketing ploy or a superficial attempt to appear socially responsible. Consumers are increasingly discerning, and they can detect inauthenticity. A genuine higher purpose arises organically from the organization's core values and reflects the genuine beliefs and motivations of its leaders and employees. This authenticity fosters trust, builds brand loyalty, and attracts employees who are genuinely aligned with the organization's mission.

Consider the example of **Patagonia,** a company whose higher purpose is deeply embedded in its operations. Patagonia's mission statement, "We're in business to save our planet," is not simply a marketing tagline; it informs every aspect of their business, from their sustainable sourcing practices to their commitment to environmental activism. Their actions consistently reflect their values, creating a powerful and authentic connection with their customers and stakeholders.

Another compelling example is TOMS Shoes, a company built around the "One for One" model. For every pair of shoes purchased, TOMS donates a pair to a child in need. This simple yet powerful model clearly articulates their higher purpose: providing essential footwear to those who lack access. Their business model is inherently linked to their social mission, creating a synergistic relationship between profit and social impact.

Conversely, companies that attempt to co-opt a higher purpose without genuine commitment risk damaging their reputation and eroding trust. "Greenwashing," the practice of making misleading or unsubstantiated claims about the environmental benefits of a product or service, is a prime example. Consumers are becoming increasingly adept at identifying such disingenuous efforts, and the consequences can be severe. Authenticity is paramount; a genuine commitment to a higher purpose must permeate every level of the organization.

Defining a company's higher purpose requires a collaborative effort involving all stakeholders. Employees should be actively involved in the process, contributing their insights and perspectives. This fosters a sense of ownership and shared responsibility, reinforcing the importance of higher purpose within the organizational culture. Regular reviews and updates ensure that the higher purpose remains relevant and adaptable to the changing context. The process shouldn't be a one-time event but an ongoing journey of reflection and refinement. As the organization evolves, its higher purpose may also need to adapt, reflecting the changing needs of the community and the evolving values of the company. This dynamic process ensures that the organization's purpose remains a guiding force, constantly inspiring growth and innovation.

The integration of a company's higher purpose into its strategic planning is paramount. It shouldn't be an afterthought but a central consideration in every decision-making process. This includes resource allocation, product development, marketing strategies, and even recruitment and employee development. All initiatives should be assessed for their alignment with the organization's higher purpose, ensuring that all actions contribute towards the overall goal.

In conclusion, defining a company's higher purpose is a transformative process. It's not just about crafting a catchy slogan or a well-intentioned statement; it's about creating a profound and lasting impact on the world. A well-defined higher purpose provides a framework for decision-making, fosters employee engagement, attracts customers and investors who share the organization's values, and ultimately builds a more resilient and sustainable business. It's about aligning profit with purpose, creating a business that is not only financially successful but also contributes meaningfully to the well-being of society and the planet. This is the essence of a truly conscious organization.

Reflection

3. Creating a Values Based Culture

Creating a values-based culture is not a mere add-on to a conscious organization; it's the very lifeblood that sustains its purpose. It's the fertile ground from which ethical decision-making sprouts, fostering an environment of trust, transparency, and accountability. This isn't achieved overnight; it requires a deliberate, ongoing commitment that permeates every aspect of the organization, from leadership styles to internal communication strategies. It's a journey, not a destination, requiring constant reflection, adaptation, and a willingness to learn and evolve.

The first crucial step is to move beyond simply stating values; they must be actively lived and embodied. A values statement plastered on a wall, untouched and unreferenced in daily operations, becomes nothing more than a hollow gesture. True integration requires a concerted effort to infuse these values into every decision, interaction, and process within the organization. This requires leadership to model the desired behavior, creating a ripple effect that permeates through the ranks.

Leaders must walk the walk, consistently demonstrating the values they espouse. This involves transparency in their actions, openness to feedback, and a commitment to ethical conduct, even when faced with difficult choices. Hypocrisy erodes trust instantaneously, creating a chasm between leadership and employees. Authenticity, in leadership and throughout the organization, is the cornerstone of a values-based culture.

This calls for a robust system of internal communication. Transparency is paramount; information must flow freely, ensuring everyone is informed and understands the rationale behind key decisions. Regular town halls, open forums, and transparent reporting mechanisms are crucial for fostering a climate of open dialogue and mutual understanding. Furthermore, mechanisms for feedback need to be established, providing safe spaces for employees to express concerns, offer suggestions, and hold the organization accountable to its stated values.

Accountability is another key component. This doesn't simply mean punishing wrongdoing; it encompasses a proactive approach to preventing ethical breaches and creating a culture where responsibility is shared. Clear guidelines, codes of conduct, and robust ethical frameworks are essential. These frameworks shouldn't be dusty tomes gathering dust on a shelf; they must be actively reviewed, updated, and integrated into employee training programs.

Regular ethical audits and internal reviews can provide valuable insights into areas needing improvement and reinforce the importance of upholding the organization's values.

Furthermore, the organization must establish mechanisms for addressing ethical dilemmas proactively. A well-defined ethical decision-making process, perhaps incorporating a formal ethics committee, allows for a structured approach to handling complex situations. This process should not only ensure compliance with legal and regulatory requirements but also provide a framework for navigating grey areas, fostering responsibility and ethical conduct even when the answer isn't immediately apparent.

Incentivizing ethical behavior is equally important. Performance reviews shouldn't solely focus on financial metrics; they must incorporate assessments of ethical conduct and alignment with organizational values. Recognizing and rewarding employees who embody the organization's values reinforces the importance of ethical behavior, creating a positive feedback loop that strengthens the values-based culture. This recognition could manifest in various ways, from public acknowledgment to performance bonuses, depending on the organization's structure and culture.

Building a values-based culture also necessitates a strong focus on employee development. Training programs should include modules on ethical decision-making, conflict resolution, and diversity and inclusion. These programs should move beyond passive learning; they need to incorporate interactive exercises, case studies, and role-playing to ensure genuine assimilation of the concepts. Furthermore, mentorship programs can be invaluable, pairing experienced employees with newer colleagues to foster a shared understanding and commitment to the organization's values.

Furthermore, the values-based culture should extend beyond the internal environment. How the organization interacts with its suppliers, customers, and the wider community is a critical reflection of its values. Fair labor practices, sustainable sourcing, and responsible environmental stewardship are all essential aspects of a truly conscious organization. This external focus reinforces the authenticity of the organization's values, creating a consistent and compelling narrative that resonates with all stakeholders.

Consider the example of a company dedicated to environmental sustainability. Their value statements might include commitments to reducing their carbon footprint, using sustainable materials, and supporting environmental conservation efforts. A truly value-based culture in such an organization would extend beyond mere lip service. It would involve meticulous tracking of energy consumption, regular reviews of their supply chain for environmentally sound practices, and active participation in environmental initiatives. This commitment would permeate every department, from product development to marketing and sales. Their commitment to sustainability wouldn't just be a marketing ploy; it would be ingrained in their daily operations.

Similarly, an organization focused on employee well-being might prioritize work-life balance, flexible working arrangements, and opportunities for professional development. This commitment wouldn't be limited to offering perks; it would involve creating a supportive work environment where employees feel valued, respected, and empowered. It would entail establishing clear boundaries between work and personal time, offering access to mental health resources, and actively promoting employee well-being through company-sponsored wellness programs. It's a holistic approach that recognizes the interconnectedness of employee well-being and organizational success.

Ultimately, creating a values-based culture is an iterative process of continuous improvement. It requires regular reflection, feedback mechanisms, and a commitment to adaptation and evolution. Values are not static; they evolve with the organization and the changing societal landscape. Regular reviews of the values statement, internal policies, and organizational practices are crucial to ensure alignment with the organization's evolving purpose and the needs of its stakeholders.

This ongoing process of refinement requires a culture of learning and adaptability. The organization should encourage experimentation, accept failures as learning opportunities, and remain open to modifying its approaches as needed. This dynamic approach ensures that the values-based culture remains relevant, resilient, and a driving force in the organization's growth and success. It's not just about creating a workplace; it's about building a community committed to a shared purpose, guided by ethical principles, and driven by a commitment to meaningful impact. This, in essence, is the foundation of a thriving conscious organization.

Reflection

4. Empowering Employees Through Purpose

Empowering employees isn't merely about offering competitive salaries and benefits; it's about igniting a fire within them, connecting their daily tasks to a larger, more meaningful purpose. This sense of purpose transcends the mundane, transforming work from a means to an end into a fulfilling and engaging experience. When employees feel their contributions matter, their productivity soars, their creativity flourishes, and their loyalty deepens. This isn't about manipulative slogans or empty corporate platitudes; it's about authentically aligning individual aspirations with the organization's overarching mission.

The journey begins with clearly articulating the organization's purpose. This isn't just a mission statement dusted off for annual reports; it's a living, breathing embodiment of the company's raison d'être. It should answer fundamental questions: What problem are we solving? What positive impact are we making on the world? How are we contributing to something larger than ourselves? This clarity allows employees to understand their role within the bigger picture, connecting their individual contributions to a collective goal.

Transparency is paramount in this process. Employees need to understand the organization's strategic goals, its challenges, and how their work directly contributes to success. Open communication channels, regular updates, and opportunities for feedback are crucial for fostering a sense of ownership and shared responsibility. This transparency fosters trust, an essential ingredient in creating a purpose-driven culture. When employees feel informed and involved, they're more likely to embrace the organization's purpose as their own.

Beyond clear communication, fostering a sense of meaning requires leadership commitment. Leaders must actively model the organization's values and purpose in their daily actions. This includes demonstrating genuine care for employees' well-being, acknowledging their contributions, and celebrating successes. It means leading by example, consistently upholding the organization's ethical standards and demonstrating a commitment to the larger purpose. Authentic leadership, rooted in empathy and integrity, is instrumental in inspiring employees to connect with the organization's mission.

Furthermore, organizations need to actively cultivate opportunities for employees to connect with the impact of their work. This might involve inviting employees to interact directly with beneficiaries of their services, sharing client testimonials highlighting the positive impact of the organization's work, or participating in volunteer projects related to the organization's purpose. These experiences create tangible links between daily tasks and the broader societal impact, fostering a deeper sense of meaning and fulfillment. Seeing the direct results of their efforts can significantly boost employee morale and motivation.

Consider Patagonia, a company renowned for its commitment to environmental sustainability. Their employees aren't just making clothing; they're contributing to a movement dedicated to protecting the planet. Patagonia actively encourages employees to participate in environmental initiatives, offers generous paid time off for volunteering, and consistently promotes environmental stewardship within their operations. This commitment isn't just a marketing ploy; it's deeply embedded in their organizational culture, fostering a profound sense of purpose among employees.

Similarly, companies focused on social impact often find that their employees are intrinsically motivated by the knowledge that their work directly improves lives. Organizations providing healthcare, education, or affordable housing, for example, tend to attract employees who are passionate about making a difference. These organizations often foster a culture of social responsibility, regularly sharing stories of the positive impact they have on individuals and communities.

However, connecting employees to a larger purpose requires more than simply stating the organization's mission. It requires actively nurturing a culture that values employee contributions and recognizes their intrinsic worth. This includes creating a supportive and inclusive work environment where everyone feels valued, respected, and empowered. It means investing in employee development, providing opportunities for growth and advancement, and offering recognition for outstanding performance.

Empowerment also extends to giving employees a voice in the organization. Encouraging open communication, active listening, and incorporating employee feedback into decision-making processes are essential for fostering a sense of ownership and engagement. This shared governance can involve creating employee task forces, soliciting input through surveys and feedback mechanisms, or implementing suggestion boxes that are actively monitored and addressed.

The impact of purpose-driven employment is substantial. Studies consistently show a strong correlation between a sense of purpose at work and increased employee engagement, productivity, and retention. Employees who feel their work is meaningful are more likely to be motivated, committed, and loyal to their organization. This, in turn, leads to improved organizational performance, profitability, and overall success. It's a win-win scenario: employees find fulfillment in their work, and the organization benefits from a highly engaged and productive workforce.

Moreover, a purpose-driven culture can attract and retain top talent. In today's competitive job market, many candidates are actively seeking organizations that align with their personal values and offer a sense of purpose beyond simply earning a paycheck. Organizations that successfully cultivate a purpose-driven culture are often able to attract and retain highly skilled and motivated employees, giving them a competitive advantage in the talent acquisition arena.

However, the journey towards creating a truly purpose-driven workplace requires sustained effort and commitment. It's not a one-time initiative but an ongoing process of reflection, adaptation, and continuous improvement. Regular assessments of employee engagement, feedback mechanisms, and ongoing refinement of the organization's purpose are crucial for maintaining a culture that effectively connects employees to a larger meaning.

The creation of a purpose-driven organization isn't about imposing a set of values from above; it's about fostering a collaborative environment where purpose is co-created and shared by all. This requires active listening, open dialogue, and a willingness to adapt and evolve as the organization and its employees grow. It's a dynamic, iterative process that requires constant attention, but the rewards—a highly engaged, productive, and purpose-driven workforce—are well worth the effort. Ultimately, empowering employees through purpose is not merely a business strategy; it's a moral imperative, creating a positive impact on both the organization and the wider world. It's about building a workplace that not only thrives economically but also contributes to a more meaningful and just society.

Reflection

5. Building Ethical Supply Chains and Partnerships

Building ethical and sustainable supply chains is no longer a "nice-to-have" but a fundamental necessity for any conscious organization. It's a reflection of the company's values, a demonstration of its commitment to social responsibility, and increasingly, a key differentiator in a market increasingly demanding transparency and accountability. This involves a multifaceted approach, demanding rigorous due diligence, a commitment to fair labor practices, and a deep understanding of the environmental impact at every stage of the supply chain.

The first step is establishing a robust due diligence process. This goes beyond simply verifying compliance with minimum legal standards. It requires a proactive and ongoing assessment of the ethical and environmental performance of every supplier, from raw material extraction to final product delivery. This involves thorough background checks, site visits (where feasible and safe), and ongoing monitoring of supplier practices. Tools like third-party audits and ethical sourcing certifications can provide valuable insights and contribute to objective assessment. However, it's crucial to remember that certifications should be viewed as a starting point, not an end goal. Direct engagement with suppliers and a willingness to address concerns collaboratively are paramount.

A critical element of ethical supply chain management is ensuring fair labor practices. This demands a commitment to paying fair wages, providing safe working conditions, respecting workers' rights, and prohibiting child labor and forced labor. Companies should develop clear codes of conduct outlining expectations for suppliers regarding labor practices, and these codes must be rigorously enforced through regular monitoring and audits. Transparency is vital; companies should be prepared to disclose information about their supply chain practices to stakeholders, demonstrating a commitment to openness and accountability.

Beyond labor standards, environmental considerations are increasingly crucial. The environmental impact of a product extends far beyond its production, encompassing raw material extraction, manufacturing, transportation, and end-of-life disposal. Companies must proactively assess the environmental footprint of their supply chain, identifying areas for improvement and implementing sustainable practices. This might involve reducing waste, promoting the use of recycled materials, optimizing transportation routes to minimize fuel consumption, and supporting suppliers who are committed to environmental stewardship. Investing in eco-friendly technologies and embracing circular economy principles can further enhance sustainability throughout the supply chain.

The transition to ethical and sustainable sourcing often involves collaborating with suppliers to support their improvement efforts. This might entail providing training on ethical labor practices, offering financial assistance to upgrade equipment or implement sustainable technologies, or sharing best practices to enhance efficiency and minimize environmental impact. Building strong, collaborative relationships with suppliers is crucial for fostering long-term sustainability. This requires a shift away from a purely transactional approach towards a partnership model that prioritizes mutual benefit and shared responsibility.

A key aspect of building ethical partnerships is establishing clear communication channels. Regular communication with suppliers ensures that expectations are understood, problems are addressed promptly, and improvements are tracked effectively. Transparency is key; suppliers need to understand the organization's values and expectations, and companies need to be open about their own challenges and limitations. This fosters trust and mutual respect, essential elements of any successful partnership.

Moreover, supporting the development of local suppliers and communities can offer numerous benefits. By investing in the growth of local businesses, companies can strengthen economic development in the regions where their products are sourced. This can lead to improved living standards, reduced poverty, and increased social stability. Supporting local farmers, artisans, and manufacturers can also contribute to biodiversity conservation and the preservation of traditional skills and knowledge. However, supporting local suppliers must be done responsibly, ensuring that they too adhere to ethical and environmental standards.

Selecting suppliers based on their ethical and environmental performance should be a key criterion in procurement decisions. This requires a more comprehensive evaluation process than simply focusing on cost and efficiency. The organization's procurement policies should explicitly reflect its commitment to ethical and sustainable sourcing, guiding decision-making throughout the procurement cycle. Regular reviews of supplier performance should be integrated into the procurement process, enabling companies to identify and address any issues promptly. Successful integration of ethical sourcing requires ongoing monitoring and evaluation. Companies should regularly assess their progress toward their sustainability goals, identify areas for improvement, and adapt their strategies accordingly. This necessitates establishing key performance indicators (KPIs) and reporting mechanisms to track progress and ensure accountability. Regular audits, both internal and external, can provide valuable insights and help identify areas where improvements are needed.

Consider companies like Patagonia, known for their commitment to Fair Trade certified cotton and their work with suppliers to reduce water usage and carbon emissions in the textile industry. They don't merely audit suppliers; they actively collaborate with them to promote sustainable practices and improve working conditions. Their approach demonstrates the power of partnership and shared responsibility in building a truly ethical supply chain. Similarly, companies like Unilever have implemented sustainable sourcing programs throughout their supply chains, focusing on issues such as deforestation, palm oil sustainability, and water stewardship. These efforts showcase the importance of integrating sustainability throughout the entire value chain.

    The journey toward building ethical and sustainable supply chains is continuous. It requires ongoing commitment, collaboration, and a willingness to adapt and improve. It's a journey that necessitates transparency, accountability, and a deep understanding of the complex social and environmental issues that impact our global supply chains. But the rewards are significant – a stronger brand reputation, improved stakeholder relations, enhanced operational efficiency, and ultimately, a positive impact on the world. This approach not only strengthens the organization's ethical foundation but also fosters innovation, enhances resilience, and contributes to a more sustainable and equitable global economy. It's an investment in the future, one that benefits the organization, its suppliers, and the communities they serve. It's a testament to the power of conscious business practices in creating a more just and sustainable world.

Reflection

6. Transparency and Accountability in Operations

Transparency and accountability are not merely buzzwords in the conscious business lexicon; they are the bedrock upon which a truly ethical and sustainable organization is built. This extends far beyond the ethical sourcing of materials discussed previously. It permeates every facet of the organization's operations, influencing everything from financial reporting to environmental disclosures and social impact assessments. A conscious organization actively embraces transparency, not as a compliance exercise, but as a strategic imperative to build trust, foster stakeholder engagement, and ultimately, drive long-term value creation.

One of the most critical areas demanding transparency is financial reporting. Beyond the legal requirements for accurate and timely financial disclosures, a conscious organization strives for greater clarity and context. This might involve providing more detailed breakdowns of revenue streams, highlighting the social and environmental impact of different business activities, and explaining the organization's financial strategy in a way that is accessible and understandable to all stakeholders, not just financial experts. Transparency in financial reporting cultivates trust and ensures that stakeholders have a clear understanding of how the organization is performing and how their investments are being used. This goes beyond simply adhering to accounting standards; it involves a proactive commitment to open communication and a willingness to engage in dialogue with stakeholders about financial matters.

Consider the growing trend towards integrated reporting, which seeks to combine financial and non-financial information into a single, holistic report. This approach acknowledges the interconnectedness of economic, environmental, and social performance and provides a more comprehensive picture of the organization's overall sustainability. By integrating social and environmental performance data into financial reporting, organizations can demonstrate the tangible link between their sustainability efforts and their financial results, strengthening their commitment to long-term value creation. This integrative approach moves beyond mere compliance and demonstrates a genuine commitment to accountability.

Environmental disclosures are another critical component of transparency in operations. A conscious organization openly shares information about its environmental footprint, including its greenhouse gas emissions, water usage, waste generation, and the overall environmental impact of its products and services. This transparency not only allows stakeholders to assess the organization's environmental performance but also allows for external scrutiny and accountability, potentially leading to improvements. The Global Reporting Initiative (GRI) provides a widely recognized framework for environmental reporting, offering a standardized approach to measuring and disclosing environmental performance. Going beyond GRI standards, however, showcases a deeper commitment to transparency and a proactive approach to environmental stewardship.

Beyond simply disclosing data, a conscious organization actively engages in dialogue with stakeholders about environmental issues. This might involve hosting public forums, participating in industry collaborations, and responding transparently to criticism or concerns. This demonstrates a willingness to learn and adapt, further building trust with stakeholders. By actively seeking feedback and engaging in open dialogue, the organization displays a level of responsiveness and commitment that goes beyond simply fulfilling disclosure requirements. This proactive engagement fosters a deeper understanding and creates space for collaborative solutions to shared environmental challenges.

Social impact assessments are an equally critical element of transparency in operations. These assessments systematically evaluate the social impacts of an organization's activities, both positive and negative, on communities, employees, and other stakeholders. This might include assessments of the organization's impact on employment, human rights, community well-being, and social equity. Transparency in this area ensures accountability and allows stakeholders to understand the organization's impact on society. A conscious organization uses this information to continuously improve its practices and minimize its negative social impacts while maximizing its positive contributions.

A crucial aspect of transparency in social impact assessment is the active engagement of communities and stakeholders affected by the organization's operations. Meaningful consultations, feedback mechanisms, and participatory decision-making processes ensure that the voices of affected stakeholders are heard and considered. This approach not only contributes to more accurate and relevant assessments but also fosters a sense of ownership and collaboration, strengthening relationships with local communities. Ignoring or neglecting stakeholder voices undermines the legitimacy of any social impact assessment. Genuine engagement fosters trust and mutual respect.

Examples of companies demonstrating exceptional levels of transparency abound. Companies like Patagonia, for instance, have long been lauded for their comprehensive sustainability reports, detailed disclosure of supply chain practices, and commitment to ethical sourcing. Their transparency extends beyond simply providing data; they proactively engage with stakeholders, actively communicate their challenges, and demonstrate a commitment to continuous improvement. Unilever, through its Sustainable Living Plan, has consistently provided transparent updates on its progress towards ambitious sustainability goals, allowing stakeholders to track the company's progress over time and hold them accountable for their commitments. Similarly, companies like Danone have adopted a holistic approach, integrating environmental, social, and governance (ESG) considerations into their financial reporting and actively promoting transparency throughout their value chain.

The journey toward greater transparency and accountability is a continuous one. It requires a deep-seated commitment to ethical values, a willingness to confront uncomfortable truths, and a genuine desire to build trust with stakeholders.

It demands ongoing evaluation, adaptation, and a commitment to learning from both successes and failures. But the rewards are substantial. Greater transparency not only builds trust and strengthens relationships with stakeholders but also fosters innovation, reduces risks, enhances efficiency, and ultimately contributes to a more sustainable and equitable global economy. It's an investment in the future, one that benefits the organization, its employees, its customers, and the communities it serves, ultimately reflecting the very essence of a conscious organization. It is a journey of continual self-reflection, a commitment to ethical practices, and a relentless pursuit of a more just and sustainable world. The conscious organization embraces this journey, not merely as a compliance exercise, but as a transformative pathway toward genuine, lasting impact.

Reflection

Chapter 7: Business as a Force for Good

1. The Pursuit of Eudaimonia Human Flourishing in the Workplace

The pursuit of profit, the traditional cornerstone of capitalism, often overlooks a critical element: the well-being of the individuals who drive the engine of commerce. While financial success remains a necessary component of any thriving business, it shouldn't come at the expense of human flourishing. This is where the ancient Greek concept of *eudaimonia*—often translated as "human flourishing" or "living well"—becomes profoundly relevant to the modern business landscape. Eudaimonia isn't simply about happiness; it's about living a life of purpose, meaning, and virtue, realizing one's full potential, and contributing positively to the world. In the context of the workplace, it translates to creating an environment where employees not only perform their tasks effectively but also experience a sense of growth, fulfillment, and overall well-being.

Integrating eudaimonia into a business model requires a fundamental shift in perspective. It demands moving beyond a purely transactional relationship with employees, viewing them not merely as cogs in a machine but as complex, multifaceted individuals with unique needs, aspirations, and potential. This shift necessitates a deep commitment to fostering a culture that values individual growth, encourages creativity, and supports employees in achieving their personal and professional goals. It's about nurturing an environment where employees feel valued, respected, and empowered to contribute their best selves to the organization. This isn't a utopian ideal; numerous organizations have already begun to demonstrate the tangible benefits of prioritizing eudaimonia. Companies that invest in employee well-being programs, such as robust mental health support, flexible work arrangements, and opportunities for professional development, often experience significant returns. Reduced employee turnover, improved productivity, increased innovation, and enhanced employee morale are just some of the observable outcomes. These companies aren't simply engaging in altruistic acts; they're recognizing the inherent link between employee well-being and organizational success. A healthy, engaged workforce is a more productive and innovative workforce, contributing directly to the bottom line.

Consider the example of companies that prioritize work-life balance. Offering flexible work arrangements, generous parental leave, and opportunities for remote work can significantly reduce employee stress and burnout. This, in turn, translates to increased productivity, reduced absenteeism, and improved job satisfaction. Furthermore, such policies attract and retain top talent, giving the company a competitive edge in a fiercely competitive job market. Employees are more likely to commit to an organization that values their well-being and respects their personal lives, fostering a culture of loyalty and dedication.

The pursuit of eudaimonia also extends to fostering a sense of purpose within the workplace. Employees are more likely to be engaged and motivated when they understand how their work contributes to a larger purpose beyond simply generating profits. Companies that articulate a strong mission statement, emphasizing their social or environmental impact, often attract individuals who are passionate about making a positive contribution to the world. This shared sense of purpose can be a powerful motivator, leading to increased creativity, innovation, and a greater willingness to go the extra mile. Employees who feel that their work is meaningful are more likely to be committed, engaged, and ultimately, more productive.

Furthermore, creating opportunities for professional development and growth is critical to fostering eudaimonia. Investing in training programs, mentoring initiatives, and opportunities for advancement can help employees acquire new skills, broaden their knowledge base, and realize their full potential. This not only benefits the individual but also enhances the organization's overall capabilities. A workforce composed of continuously learning and growing individuals is better equipped to adapt to changing market conditions and meet emerging challenges. This commitment to employee growth underscores the organization's commitment to the well-being and success of its people, fostering a virtuous cycle of mutual benefit.

The benefits of prioritizing eudaimonia extend beyond the immediate workforce. A company committed to employee well-being often enjoys a stronger reputation and enhanced brand image. Customers are increasingly drawn to organizations that demonstrate a commitment to ethical and sustainable practices, including prioritizing employee well-being. This positive brand image can enhance customer loyalty and attract new customers who share the company's values. Such a commitment is not simply a feel-good gesture; it is a strategic advantage that strengthens the company's position in the market and fosters long-term sustainability.

However, integrating eudaimonia into a business model is not without its challenges. Measuring the impact of well-being initiatives can be complex, requiring sophisticated metrics beyond simple profit margins. Furthermore, implementing these initiatives requires a significant investment of time, resources, and a commitment to cultural

change within the organization. Leadership plays a crucial role in fostering a culture that embraces eudaimonia, modeling the desired behaviors and creating systems that support employee well-being. This may involve overcoming resistance from traditional management styles that prioritize short-term gains over long-term employee development and satisfaction.

The successful integration of eudaimonia requires a holistic approach, considering not just individual well-being but also the organizational context. This involves creating a supportive work environment that fosters collaboration, open communication, and a sense of community. It requires investing in systems that promote mental health, prevent burnout, and encourage work-life integration. It necessitates a long-term vision that recognizes the interconnectedness of employee well-being, organizational success, and societal impact.

In conclusion, the pursuit of eudaimonia – human flourishing– is not merely a noble aspiration but a strategic imperative for businesses seeking long-term success and sustainability. By prioritizing employee well-being, fostering a sense of purpose, and investing in individual growth, companies can create a more engaged, productive, and innovative workforce. This, in turn, translates to enhanced profitability, a stronger brand image, and a positive contribution to society. The integration of eudaimonia represents a paradigm shift in how we understand and define success in the modern business world, moving beyond a narrow focus on profit to embrace a more holistic vision of human flourishing and organizational prosperity. It's a path that promises not only financial success but also a more meaningful and fulfilling experience for all stakeholders. This is the essence of conscious capitalism – a model where profit and purpose, individual well-being and organizational success, are inextricably intertwined, creating a more sustainable and equitable future for both business and humanity.

Reflection

2. Embracing Interconnectedness in Supply Chains

The concept of *eudaimonia,* the pursuit of human flourishing, extends far beyond the internal operations of a business and deeply impacts its external relationships, particularly within its supply chain. A truly conscious business recognizes that its success is inextricably linked to the well-being of every individual and ecosystem touched by its operations. This interconnectedness demands a radical re-evaluation of traditional supply chain management, shifting from a purely transactional model to one built on ethical partnerships, transparency, and shared prosperity.

The traditional approach to supply chain management often prioritizes cost minimization above all else. This frequently leads to exploitative labor practices, environmental degradation, and a lack of accountability throughout the supply chain. Businesses might source materials from factories with poor working conditions, ignoring the human cost of cheap production. They may choose suppliers who engage in unsustainable practices, contributing to environmental damage and resource depletion. This narrow focus on profit maximization, neglecting the broader social and environmental consequences, is fundamentally incompatible with the principles of conscious capitalism and the pursuit of eudaimonia.

Embracing interconnectedness in the supply chain requires a paradigm shift, prioritizing ethical sourcing, fair labor practices, and environmental sustainability as core elements of the business model. This means actively engaging with suppliers to understand their operations, ensuring compliance with ethical and environmental standards, and fostering mutually beneficial relationships built on trust and transparency. It's about recognizing that the success of the business is dependent on the success of its suppliers, and vice versa.

One crucial aspect of this approach is the implementation of rigorous due diligence processes. Businesses must conduct thorough audits of their suppliers, verifying their adherence to ethical labor standards, environmental regulations, and other relevant criteria. This involves more than simply checking boxes on a compliance checklist; it requires a genuine commitment to understanding the realities of the supply chain and addressing any identified issues proactively. This might involve working with suppliers to improve their working conditions, providing training on sustainable practices, and offering financial support to facilitate improvements.

Transparency is another critical element of an interconnected supply chain. Businesses should strive to provide consumers with clear and accurate information about the origin of their products, the conditions under which they were produced, and the environmental impact of their production. This transparency builds trust with consumers, enhances brand reputation, and fosters a sense of shared responsibility. Technologies such as blockchain can play a vital role in enhancing transparency by providing a secure and verifiable record of the entire supply chain, from raw material sourcing to final product delivery.

Beyond simply complying with minimum ethical and environmental standards, conscious businesses often actively seek to exceed expectations, working with suppliers to promote continuous improvement. This might involve supporting supplier development programs, providing technical assistance, and fostering innovation in sustainable production methods. The goal is not simply to meet minimum standards but to create a positive feedback loop, where both the business and its suppliers benefit from a commitment to ethical and sustainable practices.

The benefits of adopting this interconnected approach to supply chain management extend beyond mere compliance and risk mitigation. By building strong, ethical relationships with suppliers, businesses create a more resilient and sustainable supply chain. This resilience is crucial in navigating unforeseen challenges, such as natural disasters, geopolitical instability, and pandemics. A network of mutually supportive partners is better equipped to withstand disruptions and maintain operations even during difficult times.

Moreover, the commitment to ethical and sustainable practices enhances brand reputation and strengthens customer loyalty. Consumers are increasingly aware of the social and environmental impact of their purchasing decisions and are more likely to support businesses that demonstrate a commitment to ethical and sustainable practices. This translates into enhanced brand equity, increased customer loyalty, and a competitive advantage in the marketplace.

Numerous successful companies have demonstrated the tangible benefits of implementing interconnected and ethical supply chain practices. Patagonia, for example, has long been recognized for its commitment to environmental sustainability and fair labor practices, sourcing materials from suppliers who share its values. Their transparency and commitment to ethical sourcing have strengthened their brand reputation and fostered strong customer loyalty. Similarly, companies such as Unilever and Starbucks have invested in supplier development programs, working with suppliers to improve their working conditions and environmental performance. These initiatives not only enhance their supply chain resilience but also improve their brand image and attract talent.

However, implementing an interconnected and ethical supply chain requires a significant investment of time, resources, and effort. It demands a commitment to long-term partnerships, a willingness to engage in challenging conversations, and a willingness to confront uncomfortable realities. It also requires a fundamental shift in mindset, moving away from a purely transactional approach to one based on collaboration, mutual respect, and shared responsibility. Leadership plays a vital role in driving this change, fostering a culture that values ethical sourcing, transparency, and sustainability throughout the organization.

Furthermore, measuring the impact of ethical and sustainable supply chain practices can be challenging. While financial metrics are often readily available, measuring the impact on social and environmental outcomes requires more sophisticated metrics and data collection methods. This might involve tracking indicators such as reduced greenhouse gas emissions, improved worker safety, or increased supplier satisfaction.

In conclusion, embracing interconnectedness in the supply chain is not merely a matter of corporate social responsibility; it's a strategic imperative for businesses seeking long-term success and sustainability. By prioritizing ethical sourcing, transparency, and collaboration, businesses can create a more resilient, sustainable, and ultimately more profitable supply chain. This approach not only benefits the business itself but also contributes to a more just and equitable global economy, aligning perfectly with the pursuit of eudaimonia for all stakeholders involved. It is a journey that requires commitment, perseverance, and a fundamental shift in how we understand the relationship between business and the wider world. This interconnectedness, viewed through the lens of quantum principles, highlights the inherent interdependence of all things, underscoring the fact that true business success is not achieved in isolation but through the flourishing of the entire ecosystem within which it operates. The ripple effect of ethical and sustainable practices extends far beyond the immediate supply chain, creating a positive impact on communities, environments, and the overall well-being of humanity.

Reflection

3. The Role of Business in Social and Environmental Change

The preceding discussion established the burgeoning landscape of conscious capitalism and the transformative trends shaping its evolution. However, the true measure of this paradigm shift lies not merely in internal corporate transformations but in the tangible impact businesses have on the broader social and environmental fabric of our world.

This section delves into the critical role businesses play in addressing some of humanity's most pressing challenges, exploring how their resources, innovation, and influence can be harnessed as powerful instruments for positive change.

Climate change, arguably the defining challenge of our time, demands a concerted global response. While governments and international organizations play a pivotal role, businesses possess the scale and resources to significantly reduce their carbon footprint and drive the transition to a low-carbon economy. This isn't solely about compliance; it represents a fundamental opportunity for innovation and competitive advantage. Companies that proactively embrace sustainability are not only mitigating their environmental impact but also tapping into a growing market for environmentally conscious products and services.

Consider the burgeoning renewable energy sector. Companies like Ørsted, once a coal-fired power giant, have successfully transitioned to become a global leader in offshore wind energy. This dramatic transformation demonstrates the potential for businesses to not only reduce their environmental footprint but also to create new economic opportunities in the process. Their commitment extends beyond simply switching energy sources; they are actively investing in research and development, fostering technological advancements, and driving down the cost of renewable energy, making it increasingly accessible and competitive. This transition not only benefits the environment but also generates new jobs, stimulates economic growth, and enhances energy security.

Beyond renewable energy, we see countless examples of businesses leading the charge in sustainable practices. Unilever, for instance, has implemented ambitious sustainability targets across its entire value chain, from sourcing raw materials to packaging and distribution. Their commitment to sustainable agriculture, responsible sourcing, and waste reduction demonstrates a holistic approach to sustainability that extends beyond mere corporate social responsibility initiatives. Their efforts, while demanding significant investment and organizational restructuring, ultimately contribute to a more resilient and sustainable business model. The success of such initiatives underscores the growing recognition that environmental sustainability is not a cost but an investment in long-term value creation.

Equally critical is the role businesses play in addressing social inequality and poverty. The disparity between the rich and poor continues to widen globally, creating significant social and economic instability. Conscious businesses can actively contribute to bridging this gap through various initiatives. Fair trade practices, ensuring fair wages and safe working conditions for suppliers and employees in developing countries, are becoming increasingly prevalent. Companies like Patagonia, renowned for their commitment to fair labor practices and environmental sustainability, demonstrate that ethical sourcing and social responsibility can coexist with profitability. Their commitment isn't simply a marketing ploy; it's deeply embedded in their company culture and values, driving their product development, supply chain management, and overall business strategy.

Furthermore, businesses can contribute to poverty reduction through job creation, skills development, and investment in local communities. Microfinance initiatives, supported by many corporations, provide access to capital for entrepreneurs in developing countries, empowering them to start and grow their businesses. This creates jobs, stimulates local economies, and contributes to broader social and economic development. Such initiatives not only alleviate poverty but also foster economic resilience and stability within communities, creating a virtuous cycle of growth and development.

The impact of conscious business practices extends beyond specific initiatives; it's about cultivating a culture of social responsibility that permeates every aspect of the business.

This involves establishing ethical guidelines, ensuring transparency and accountability across the supply chain, and actively engaging stakeholders in decision-making processes. It requires a shift from a purely profit-maximizing mindset to a more holistic approach that considers the social and environmental consequences of business decisions.

The adoption of ESG (Environmental, Social, and Governance) reporting frameworks is becoming increasingly commonplace, providing greater transparency and accountability for businesses. These reports provide stakeholders with a comprehensive overview of a company's social and environmental performance, enabling informed investment decisions and fostering greater trust and engagement. While initially driven by regulatory pressures and investor demand, ESG reporting is increasingly recognized as a valuable tool for internal improvement and strategic decision-making. By systematically tracking and analyzing their social and environmental impact, businesses can identify areas for improvement, optimize their operations, and demonstrate their commitment to sustainability.

Moreover, the increasing influence of investing is accelerating the shift towards conscious capitalism. Impact investors prioritize both financial returns and positive social and environmental impact, driving significant investments in companies committed to sustainability and social responsibility. This infusion of capital provides crucial resources for growth and expansion, empowering conscious businesses to scale their operations and amplify their positive impact. The growth of impact investing underscores the growing recognition that financial success and social progress are not mutually exclusive but rather intertwined and mutually reinforcing.

However, the integration of social and environmental responsibility into business operations isn't without its challenges. Measuring and reporting on social and environmental impact can be complex and require significant resources. Supply chain transparency can be difficult to achieve, particularly in globalized industries. Balancing competing stakeholder interests requires careful consideration and effective communication. Overcoming these challenges demands a commitment to innovation, collaboration, and a willingness to embrace new approaches and technologies.

Technology plays an increasingly important role in driving positive changes. Blockchain technology, for example, enhances supply chain traceability, enabling businesses to monitor and improve labor practices, environmental impact, and product sourcing. AI and machine learning can optimize resource allocation, reduce waste, and improve efficiency, minimizing the environmental footprint of business operations. Data analytics provides insights into social and environmental performance, enabling data-driven decision-making and more effective impact measurement. The adoption of these technologies is not simply about improving efficiency; it is about fundamentally transforming how businesses operate, fostering a more responsible and sustainable approach to production and distribution.

In conclusion, the role of businesses in social and environmental change is paramount. By leveraging their resources, innovation, and influence, companies can significantly contribute to addressing global challenges such as climate change, inequality, and poverty. The examples provided demonstrate the tangible impact of conscious business practices and highlight the growing recognition that financial success and social progress are inextricably linked.

    The path towards a more sustainable and equitable future requires a fundamental shift in mindset, a commitment to collaboration, and a willingness to embrace innovation and new technologies. The time for conscious capitalism is now; it is not merely a trend but a necessary transformation for a prosperous and sustainable future for all. The integration of social and environmental considerations into core business strategies is not merely ethical; it is a strategic imperative for long-term success and a critical contribution to the well-being of our planet and its people. The future belongs to those businesses that understand and embrace this fundamental truth.

Reflection

4. Building a Sustainable and Regenerative Economy

The preceding discussion highlighted the crucial role of conscious businesses in addressing pressing social and environmental issues. However, the journey towards a truly sustainable future necessitates a deeper transformation— a shift from a linear "take-make-dispose" economic model to a circular, regenerative one. This transition is not merely an environmental imperative; it's a fundamental reimagining of how we create, distribute, and consume goods and services, creating a more resilient and equitable economy for all.

The core principle of a circular economy is to eliminate waste and pollution. Instead of extracting resources, manufacturing products, and discarding them after use, the circular model emphasizes keeping materials in use for as long as possible, extracting maximum value from them, and then recovering and regenerating them at the end of their service life. This fundamentally differs from the traditional linear model, which relies on constant resource extraction and waste generation. In essence, it's a shift from a system of depletion to one of renewal.

Consider the example of clothing. In a linear economy, clothes are manufactured, worn, and then discarded, often ending up in landfills. This process contributes to pollution from textile production, resource depletion, and environmental damage from waste disposal. A circular approach, however, might involve using recycled materials in clothing production, extending the life of garments through repair and reuse initiatives, and developing innovative recycling technologies to recover valuable fibers from discarded clothing. Companies like Patagonia are leading the way in this area, actively promoting repair services, encouraging clothing reuse, and even offering a program to take back worn-out garments for recycling.

This concept extends far beyond the clothing industry. The construction industry, for example, could drastically reduce its environmental impact by employing modular designs that facilitate easy disassembly and reuse of building materials. Innovative companies are exploring the use of bio-based materials and construction techniques that minimize environmental footprints and prioritize the use of recycled or reclaimed materials. This approach not only reduces waste but also creates new opportunities for innovation and the development of sustainable building practices.

The food industry represents another area ripe for transformation. Reducing food waste is a critical step towards a more sustainable food system. Initiatives aimed at improving supply chain efficiency, promoting responsible consumption habits, and developing innovative solutions for food waste management are crucial for building a truly circular food system. Companies are increasingly exploring solutions such as composting, anaerobic digestion, and the development of food products made from by-products or surplus food.

The transition to a circular economy requires a fundamental shift in business models. It necessitates a move away from solely focusing on product sales towards offering services and solutions. Instead of selling products, businesses can offer product-as-a-service models, retaining ownership of the products and responsible for their maintenance and eventual recycling or reuse. This shifts the focus from maximizing sales to maximizing product lifespan and resource utilization, creating a fundamentally different value proposition. This also incentivizes the design of durable, repairable, and recyclable products, contributing to a reduction in waste and resource consumption.

Technological innovation is pivotal to enabling the transition to a circular economy. Blockchain technology, for instance, can enhance traceability of materials, ensuring responsible sourcing and minimizing the risk of using materials from unsustainable sources. Artificial intelligence (AI) and machine learning can optimize resource allocation, improve efficiency in manufacturing processes, and facilitate the development of more effective recycling technologies. The application of these technologies isn't simply about improving efficiency; it is about fundamentally transforming the way businesses operate and interact with the environment.

   Furthermore, achieving a regenerative economy requires businesses to move beyond simply reducing their negative impact to actively restoring ecological balance. This means actively contributing to environmental restoration, biodiversity conservation, and carbon sequestration. Companies can achieve this through various initiatives, such as investing in reforestation projects, supporting sustainable agriculture practices, or developing products that have a positive environmental impact. These actions demonstrate a commitment to going beyond sustainability and actively contributing to the regeneration of natural systems.

   The financial sector also has a significant role to play in supporting the transition to a circular economy. Impact investing is increasingly focusing on businesses that operate within a circular model, providing capital for innovative solutions and driving the adoption of sustainable business practices. Green bonds and other sustainable finance instruments are also playing an increasingly important role in financing projects that contribute to the transition to a circular economy.

   The challenges in creating a circular economy are considerable. It requires collaboration across various sectors, significant investment in new technologies and infrastructure, and a shift in consumer behavior. However, the potential benefits are immense—a more resilient economy, reduced environmental damage, improved resource efficiency, and new opportunities for innovation and job creation. The journey towards a circular and regenerative economy is not a sprint but a marathon, requiring long-term commitment and sustained effort from businesses, governments, and individuals alike. It is a transformative shift that will require a complete rethinking of economic systems and business models. However, the ultimate reward is a more sustainable, equitable, and prosperous future for generations to come. It's a future where business success is inextricably linked to planetary well-being, where economic growth and environmental restoration coexist and flourish. This is not just a vision; it is a necessity, and it is within our collective reach. The question is not whether we can achieve it, but whether we will choose to. The path forward is clear: embrace the circular economy, foster regenerative practices, and build a future where economic prosperity is deeply intertwined with ecological health. This is the future of conscious business, a future where profit and purpose are no longer separate but are deeply intertwined aspects of a thriving and sustainable enterprise. The path ahead demands innovation, collaboration, and unwavering commitment. But the destination—a truly sustainable and regenerative economy—is worth the journey.

Reflection

5. Inspiring the Next Generation of Conscious Leaders

The preceding chapters have established the foundational principles of conscious business and the imperative for a shift towards a circular, regenerative economy. However, the sustainability of this transformation hinges on a critical element: the next generation of leaders. Building a truly conscious future requires cultivating a new breed of business professionals who deeply understand and embody the principles of ethical leadership, sustainable practices, and the interconnectedness of profit and purpose. This is not merely a matter of imparting knowledge; it's about fostering a fundamental shift in mindset and values.

The current educational landscape, while evolving, often lags behind the urgent need for conscious leadership. Traditional MBA programs, while valuable for developing business acumen, frequently fall short in integrating ethical considerations and holistic sustainability into the core curriculum. The focus often remains narrowly defined on maximizing shareholder value, often neglecting the broader social and environmental implications of business decisions. This creates a disconnect between the realities of a complex, interconnected world and the training provided to aspiring business leaders.

To address this gap, a transformative shift in leadership development is required. This necessitates integrating ethics, sustainability, and social responsibility into the very fabric of business education. This isn't simply about adding a few elective courses on environmental sustainability or corporate social responsibility; it's about embedding these principles throughout the curriculum, from foundational business principles to strategic decision-making. A holistic approach is crucial, emphasizing the interconnectedness of environmental, social, and economic considerations. Future leaders need to understand not just how to generate profits but also how to generate positive social and environmental impact.

This requires a fundamental reevaluation of the metrics used to assess leadership success. Moving beyond traditional metrics like profitability and market share, we must incorporate indicators that reflect the social and environmental impact of a business. This could include metrics such as carbon footprint reduction, employee well-being, community engagement, and ethical sourcing practices. By incorporating these measures into leadership evaluations, we incentivize leaders to prioritize a wider range of values, moving beyond a narrow focus on pure financial success.

Mentorship plays a crucial role in this transformation. Experienced leaders who embody the principles of conscious business can serve as invaluable guides for aspiring professionals. This mentorship should go beyond simply providing career advice; it should involve sharing personal experiences, offering ethical guidance, and helping younger leaders navigate complex moral dilemmas. Experienced leaders can provide invaluable insights into the challenges and rewards of integrating ethical considerations into business strategy. To effectively cultivate conscious leaders, a robust ecosystem of support is essential. This includes creating opportunities for networking and collaboration among conscious business leaders, facilitating knowledge sharing and mutual support. Professional organizations and industry groups can play a significant role in establishing these networks, creating platforms for exchanging best practices and fostering a sense of shared purpose.

Universities and business schools must take a proactive role in designing curricula that reflect the evolving needs of the conscious business world. Integrating case studies showcasing companies that successfully integrate ethical and sustainable practices is crucial. This allows future leaders to learn from the successes and failures of companies that have embraced conscious business models, providing practical insights and valuable lessons.

Furthermore, experiential learning is vital. Opportunities for internships and fieldwork at conscious businesses provide invaluable hands-on experience, allowing students to apply theoretical knowledge to real-world contexts. This immersive learning approach not only deepens their understanding of conscious business principles but also provides them with valuable skills and networks that will benefit them throughout their careers.

Beyond formal educational institutions, the role of lifelong learning cannot be overstated. Conscious leadership is an ongoing journey of growth and development. Leaders must continuously seek opportunities to expand their knowledge and skills, stay abreast of evolving best practices, and adapt to changing circumstances. This continuous learning process ensures that leaders remain relevant and effective in a rapidly changing business environment.

The integration of spirituality and mindfulness practices can significantly enhance the development of conscious leaders. Mindfulness training, for example, can help leaders develop greater self-awareness, emotional intelligence, and ethical decision-making skills. By incorporating these practices into leadership development programs, we cultivate leaders who are not only competent but also compassionate, resilient, and deeply connected to their values.

It's crucial to acknowledge that fostering a generation of conscious leaders isn't solely the responsibility of educational institutions. Businesses themselves must play an active role in cultivating this leadership pipeline. Companies should implement comprehensive training programs that focus on ethical decision-making, sustainability practices, and social responsibility. Investing in employee development is not only ethically responsible but also strategically advantageous, leading to increased employee engagement, enhanced brand reputation, and improved long-term sustainability.

Government policies can also play a vital role in supporting the development of conscious leaders. Incentivizing businesses to invest in employee training programs, promoting ethical sourcing and sustainable practices, and supporting educational initiatives focused on conscious leadership can create a favorable environment for the growth of conscious businesses and the development of a new generation of leaders.

The development of ethical frameworks for leadership is crucial. These frameworks shouldn't merely be abstract principles; they should be practical tools that guide decision-making in complex business contexts. These frameworks should incorporate principles of fairness, transparency, accountability, and sustainability. They should also address issues such as conflict of interest, ethical dilemmas, and the responsible use of technology. By providing concrete guidelines and practical tools, we can equip leaders with the resources they need to make ethical decisions consistently.

The transition to a truly conscious and sustainable future depends on the leadership of tomorrow. By investing in the education, training, and mentorship of future generations of conscious leaders, we are not just building a more sustainable economy; we are cultivating a more just and equitable world. This requires a collaborative effort among businesses, educational institutions, governments, and individuals, all working together towards a common vision of a thriving and sustainable future. This is an investment not only in the future of business but also in the future of humanity. The journey requires commitment, collaboration, and unwavering dedication to fostering ethical leadership, responsible practices, and a deep understanding of the interconnectedness of economic prosperity, social justice, and environmental sustainability. The future of business, and indeed the planet, depends on it.

Reflection

6. Cultivating a Culture of Purpose and Meaning

Cultivating a thriving business in the 21st century demands more than just financial success; it requires a deep-seated commitment to purpose and meaning. This isn't merely a feel-good exercise; it's a fundamental shift in organizational philosophy, reflecting the interconnectedness inherent in quantum principles. A culture infused with purpose and meaning directly impacts employee engagement, productivity, and ultimately, the long-term sustainability of the business. It fosters a sense of shared identity and collective responsibility, transforming the workplace from a mere source of income to a platform for personal and professional growth.

The starting point lies in articulating a compelling and authentic organizational purpose that extends beyond profit maximization. This purpose should resonate with employees on a deeply personal level, connecting their individual aspirations with the company's overarching mission. It's about defining "why" the business exists, what positive impact it strives to make on the world, and how it intends to achieve this impact. This isn't just a marketing slogan; it's the guiding principle that shapes every decision, from product development to internal policy. Consider companies like Patagonia, whose commitment to environmental sustainability isn't just a marketing ploy but a core value integrated into every aspect of their operations. Their purpose resonates deeply with employees who share a passion for environmental protection, fostering a highly engaged and motivated workforce.

Beyond the articulation of purpose, fostering a sense of belonging is paramount. Employees need to feel valued, respected, and heard – not simply as cogs in a machine, but as integral members of a community. This requires creating an inclusive environment where diversity is celebrated, and individuals feel safe to express their unique perspectives and experiences. Initiatives such as employee resource groups, mentorship programs, and open communication channels can facilitate this sense of belonging. Regular feedback mechanisms, allowing employees to share their thoughts and concerns, are crucial. This fosters psychological safety, enabling employees to feel comfortable contributing their ideas and openly voicing concerns, thereby creating a more collaborative and innovative work environment. Furthermore, a strong organizational culture promotes a sense of psychological safety, where employees feel comfortable taking risks, sharing their ideas, and openly expressing concerns without fear of retribution.

Alignment between individual and organizational goals is another key component of a purpose-driven culture. Employees need to understand how their daily tasks contribute to the broader mission. This requires clear communication and regular reinforcement of the company's values and goals. Managers play a crucial role in this process, connecting individual responsibilities with the overall organizational purpose. Providing opportunities for professional development and skill enhancement not only benefits employees but also aligns individual growth aspirations with the company's needs. This fosters a sense of ownership and commitment, turning employees into active participants in the company's success story. Furthermore, leadership development programs are crucial to ensure that managers can effectively communicate the organizational purpose and foster a culture of engagement and belonging.

Building a culture of purpose and meaning also necessitates transparent and ethical business practices. Employees are increasingly drawn to organizations that operate with integrity and social responsibility. Transparency in decision-making, fair compensation and benefits, and a commitment to environmental sustainability are vital aspects of building trust and fostering a positive work environment. This transparency extends to how the organization engages with its supply chain and interacts with its communities. Regular communication regarding ethical considerations builds trust, strengthens employee engagement, and enhances the company's reputation.

Investing in employee well-being is another critical element. A holistic approach recognizes that employees are more than just workers; they are individuals with lives outside the workplace. Supporting their physical, mental, and emotional health leads to increased productivity, reduced stress, and a more positive work environment. This may involve offering wellness programs, flexible work arrangements, and ample opportunities for rest and rejuvenation. Beyond the tangible benefits, this investment demonstrates genuine care for employees, fostering a sense of loyalty and commitment.

Measuring the impact of culture-building initiatives requires a shift from traditional metrics to a more holistic approach. While financial performance remains important, a purpose-driven organization also tracks employee engagement, satisfaction, retention rates, and measures of social and environmental impact. These metrics provide a more complete picture of the organization's success, reflecting its commitment to its employees and the wider community.

Regular employee surveys and feedback mechanisms provide valuable insights into the effectiveness of culture-building initiatives and areas for improvement. Moreover, fostering a culture of continuous learning and improvement is essential. A quantum approach emphasizes adaptability and a willingness to embrace change. Regular training and development opportunities equip employees with the skills and knowledge necessary to navigate a rapidly evolving business landscape. Creating a culture of experimentation and learning from mistakes fosters innovation and resilience. Employees should feel empowered to challenge existing practices, propose new ideas, and contribute to the organization's ongoing evolution. This creates a dynamic and engaging environment where employees are actively involved in shaping the company's future.

The integration of spirituality into the workplace, while not universally embraced, can significantly contribute to a culture of purpose and meaning. This doesn't necessarily mean imposing religious beliefs, but rather incorporating principles of mindfulness, compassion, and ethical conduct into the organizational culture. Mindfulness practices, such as meditation or yoga, can reduce stress, enhance focus, and promote a more harmonious work environment. A focus on compassion and empathy fosters a culture of understanding and respect, building stronger relationships between employees and fostering collaboration. Ethical considerations, aligned with a broader sense of purpose, guide decision-making, building a stronger sense of trust and integrity.

Ultimately, cultivating a culture of purpose and meaning is an ongoing journey, not a destination. It requires consistent effort, commitment, and a willingness to adapt and evolve. It's a process of continuous learning, refinement, and reflection. By embracing a holistic approach, integrating quantum principles of interconnectedness, and focusing on employee well-being, organizations can create a thriving culture that fosters engagement, innovation, and long-term sustainability. This journey transforms the business into a force for positive change, benefiting not only its employees and stakeholders but also the wider world. It's a testament to the power of aligning business with purpose, creating a legacy that extends far beyond the balance sheet. The ripple effects of such a culture are profound, resonating throughout the organization, the community, and the global ecosystem. The investment in cultivating this kind of culture is not an expense, but a strategic advantage that yields significant returns in terms of employee loyalty, productivity, and long-term growth.

Reflection

Chapter 8: Case Studies in Conscious Business

1. Patagonia A Model of Conscious Capitalism

Patagonia's journey stands as a compelling example of conscious capitalism, a model that transcends the traditional profit-maximizing paradigm by prioritizing environmental and social responsibility alongside financial success. Founded by Yvon Chouinard, a passionate climber and environmentalist, Patagonia has consistently interwoven its values into its business strategy, demonstrating that profitability and ethical conduct are not mutually exclusive. Their commitment to sustainability isn't merely a marketing ploy; it's deeply ingrained in their operations, from sourcing materials to manufacturing processes and product design.

The company's dedication to environmental conservation is perhaps its most striking characteristic. Patagonia actively campaigns for the protection of wild spaces, contributing significantly to environmental organizations and advocating for policies that promote sustainability. This commitment extends beyond donations; it informs their product lifecycle, prioritizing the use of recycled materials, minimizing waste, and promoting durable, repairable products to reduce consumption. Their "Worn Wear" program, encouraging customers to repair and reuse their clothing, exemplifies this commitment, directly countering the fast-fashion industry's culture of disposability. This initiative not only reduces waste but also fosters a sense of community and longevity associated with their brand. It's a conscious decision to prioritize the planet over short-term profit, a move that resonates deeply with their environmentally conscious customer base.

Furthermore, Patagonia's commitment to fair labor practices is equally significant. They meticulously scrutinize their supply chains, ensuring ethical sourcing and fair wages for workers throughout their manufacturing process. Transparency is paramount in their approach; they publicly disclose information about their suppliers, allowing customers to understand the origins of their products and the conditions under which they are made. This transparency builds trust with consumers and holds their suppliers accountable, promoting ethical and responsible manufacturing practices across the industry. The company's commitment goes beyond merely complying with labor laws; it actively strives to exceed standards, creating a ripple effect that encourages similar practices within their industry.

Beyond its environmental and social commitments, Patagonia's organizational culture reflects its conscious capitalism philosophy. Employee empowerment and a strong sense of purpose are central to their approach. Employees are encouraged to contribute to environmental causes, and the company actively promotes volunteerism and community engagement. This fostering of a shared purpose not only boosts employee morale and engagement but also aligns individual aspirations with the company's broader mission. It cultivates a sense of belonging and shared responsibility, creating a highly motivated and engaged workforce. This commitment to employee well-being extends beyond simply offering competitive salaries and benefits; it fosters a sense of purpose and shared values, attracting and retaining top talent who are drawn to the company's ethical and sustainable mission.

One of the key lessons from Patagonia's success is the power of aligning business goals with core values. Their commitment to sustainability and fair labor practices isn't an afterthought; it's integral to their brand identity and a driving force behind their business strategy. This alignment resonates deeply with their target audience, fostering brand loyalty and creating a strong competitive advantage. This intrinsic connection between values and operations demonstrates that businesses can thrive while operating ethically and responsibly. It's a powerful example of how a conscious business model can not only be successful but can also inspire positive change within an industry and beyond.

However, Patagonia's journey isn't without its challenges. Balancing environmental concerns with the demands of a global market presents constant complexities. The cost of sustainable materials can be higher than traditional alternatives and navigating complex supply chains to ensure ethical labor practices requires ongoing vigilance and investment. Maintaining transparency and accountability requires significant resources and a commitment to ongoing scrutiny. This level of commitment demands continuous effort and adaptation, highlighting the need for long-term vision and a willingness to confront difficult decisions. Their success demonstrates the dedication required to navigate these hurdles and maintain their commitment to ethical and sustainable practices.

The company's approach to marketing and communication also deserves attention. Patagonia avoids manipulative advertising tactics, instead focusing on authentic storytelling and transparent communication. They highlight the environmental and social impact of their products and openly address the challenges they face in their sustainability efforts. This honesty fosters trust and builds a strong connection with consumers who value authenticity and transparency. This approach demonstrates that marketing can be ethical and impactful, focusing on building relationships with consumers based on shared values rather than manipulating consumer desire.

Furthermore, Patagonia's success highlights the importance of long-term vision and strategic planning. Their commitment to sustainability is not a fleeting trend; it's a fundamental aspect of their long-term business strategy. This long-term perspective allows them to make strategic investments in sustainable materials, technologies, and ethical supply chains, even when the short-term costs might be higher. This patience and dedication demonstrate that conscious capitalism is a long-term investment that yields significant returns not just financially but also in terms of social and environmental impact.

Patagonia's model offers valuable insights for other businesses seeking to integrate conscious principles into their operations. The key takeaway is the importance of aligning values with business strategy, fostering a culture of transparency and accountability, and prioritizing long-term sustainability over short-term gains. It's a testament to the potential for businesses to thrive while simultaneously contributing to a more just and sustainable world. Their success isn't solely about financial profits; it's about creating a positive impact, demonstrating that conscious capitalism can be a powerful force for change.

The challenge for other businesses lies in understanding that integrating conscious principles isn't a mere add-on; it requires a fundamental shift in mindset and a commitment to long-term vision. It involves a willingness to invest in sustainable practices, even when short-term costs might be higher, and a commitment to transparency and accountability throughout the supply chain. It requires a deep understanding of the social and environmental impacts of business operations and a willingness to address those impacts proactively. This transformation demands strong leadership, a dedicated team, and a commitment to continuous improvement.

For businesses seeking to emulate Patagonia's model, a crucial starting point is to identify their core values and ensure that these values are genuinely reflected in every aspect of their operations, from product design and sourcing to employee relations and marketing. Regularly assessing their social and environmental impact is crucial, allowing for adjustments and improvements in their practices. Engaging with stakeholders—including employees, suppliers, customers, and the wider community—is also essential for fostering transparency and accountability. Patagonia's journey serves as a roadmap, demonstrating that conscious capitalism isn't just a theoretical concept but a viable and successful business model that can create positive change while achieving long-term profitability. The journey requires continuous effort, adaptation, and a steadfast commitment to aligning values with business practices. Ultimately, it's a testament to the powerful potential of conscious capitalism to reshape the business landscape and create a more sustainable and equitable future.

Reflection

2. Unilever's Sustainable Living Plan

Unilever, a multinational consumer goods giant, offers a contrasting yet equally compelling case study in conscious business practices. While Patagonia's focus is on a niche market with a strong environmental ethos, Unilever's ambition is far broader, aiming to integrate sustainability into its vast and diverse portfolio of brands, impacting billions of consumers globally. Their Sustainable Living Plan (USLP), launched in 2010, represents a bold attempt to reconcile profit maximization with a commitment to environmental and social responsibility on an unprecedented scale. This plan set ambitious targets across three key pillars: improving health and well-being, reducing environmental impact, and enhancing livelihoods.

The USLP wasn't merely a public relations exercise; it was deeply embedded within Unilever's strategic framework, influencing product development, supply chain management, and marketing strategies. The company aimed to decouple its growth from its environmental footprint, aiming for a significant reduction in greenhouse gas emissions, water usage, and waste generation, while simultaneously increasing the positive social impact of its operations. This required a substantial shift in mindset, demanding investment in research and development, supply chain redesign, and extensive employee training.

One of the key strategies within the USLP was the development and promotion of sustainable brands. Unilever identified several of its brands – Dove, Lifebuoy, and Persil, among others – as vehicles for delivering positive social and environmental impact. Dove's commitment to promoting real beauty and body positivity became a powerful marketing tool, resonating with consumers and strengthening brand loyalty. Lifebuoy's focus on hygiene and handwashing in developing countries addressed crucial public health issues while also boosting sales. Persil's focus on developing more environmentally friendly cleaning products demonstrated the company's commitment to reducing its impact on the environment. This brand-specific approach allowed Unilever to target different sustainability goals using the unique strengths and market positions of its brands.

The USLP also entailed a significant overhaul of Unilever's supply chain. The company recognized that a substantial portion of its environmental and social footprint stemmed from its sourcing and manufacturing processes. This led to initiatives to source sustainable palm oil, reduce water usage in its factories, and improve working conditions for agricultural workers in its supply chain. This commitment involved collaborating with suppliers, NGOs, and other stakeholders to establish ethical and sustainable practices throughout the entire value chain. This wasn't a simple task; it required significant investment, complex negotiations, and a long-term commitment to building trust and collaboration with a vast network of suppliers across the globe.

Unilever's progress towards its USLP goals has been significant, albeit with challenges. The company made measurable strides in reducing its environmental footprint, such as lowering greenhouse gas emissions and water usage. It also improved the livelihoods of millions of people through various initiatives, such as promoting sustainable agriculture and empowering women in its supply chains. However, the path to achieving its ambitious targets has not been without setbacks. The complexity of managing a global supply chain, the challenges of transitioning to more sustainable materials and processes, and the inherent difficulties in quantifying and measuring the social impact of its initiatives all presented significant hurdles.

The USLP faced external scrutiny as well. Critics questioned the authenticity of Unilever's commitment, suggesting that some initiatives were primarily for marketing purposes. Others raised concerns about the adequacy of the targets set and the transparency of its reporting. These criticisms highlight the challenges inherent in balancing corporate social responsibility with the demands of a competitive global market. A company of Unilever's scale will always be subject to scrutiny and debate around its actions.

One of the key lessons emerging from Unilever's experience with the USLP is the importance of setting clear, measurable, achievable, relevant, and time-bound (SMART) goals. While ambitious targets can inspire innovation and drive progress, they also need to be realistic and achievable given the company's resources and operational capabilities. Unilever's experience underscores the need for a carefully phased approach, allowing for adjustments and refinements along the way.

Furthermore, Unilever's case demonstrates the crucial role of stakeholder engagement. Effective collaboration with suppliers, NGOs, consumers, and governments is essential for achieving meaningful progress on sustainability initiatives. Unilever's success, to the extent it has been successful, reflects its ability to build strong relationships and foster trust with these stakeholders, generating collective action toward shared goals.

The transparency of reporting is another crucial factor. The public scrutiny facing Unilever highlights the importance of open and honest communication about its progress, challenges, and setbacks. This transparency not only builds trust with consumers and stakeholders but also enables continuous improvement by allowing for external feedback and assessment.

In conclusion, Unilever's Sustainable Living Plan serves as a complex and nuanced case study in conscious business practices. While not without its shortcomings and criticisms, the initiative represents a significant attempt by a major multinational corporation to integrate sustainability into its core business strategy. Its successes and failures offer invaluable lessons for other businesses seeking to embrace a more conscious and sustainable approach to business. The scale of Unilever's undertaking highlights the challenges and opportunities inherent in achieving large-scale positive social and environmental impact. The company's journey underscores the need for long-term commitment, strategic planning, robust stakeholder engagement, and transparent communication as essential components of any successful sustainability initiative. The ongoing evolution of the USLP, and its successor initiatives, continue to provide a rich field of study for those exploring the intersection of business and sustainability. The long-term impacts of Unilever's efforts will be measured for years to come, offering continued insights into the possibilities and pitfalls of integrating conscious principles into a global business operation. The critical evaluation of their methodology and results offers valuable lessons for future endeavors in this arena, proving that the journey towards conscious capitalism is an ongoing process of adaptation, learning, and commitment. The inherent complexities involved in scaling sustainable practices across a vast global operation, managing diverse stakeholder expectations, and navigating evolving regulatory landscapes offer a valuable case study for future business leaders seeking to make a meaningful contribution to a more sustainable future. The ongoing dialogue and scrutiny surrounding Unilever's sustainability efforts highlight the importance of continuous learning, adaptation, and transparency in the pursuit of a truly conscious business model. Their story, both in successes and setbacks, provides a valuable roadmap and cautionary tale for others on this challenging yet vital journey.

Reflection

3. Seventh Generation Environmental Sustainability in Action

Seventh Generation's journey exemplifies a deep commitment to environmental sustainability, extending far beyond a simple marketing ploy. Unlike many companies that adopt green initiatives as a superficial add-on, Seventh Generation has woven environmental consciousness into the very fabric of its existence, from product conception to end-of-life disposal. This holistic approach, coupled with transparent communication and a proactive engagement with environmental concerns, positions them as a leader in the conscious business movement. Their success underscores the fact that environmental responsibility isn't just a cost; it can be a significant competitive advantage and a powerful driver of brand loyalty.

The company's commitment begins with its product formulations. Seventh Generation rigorously researches and selects ingredients with minimal environmental impact. This goes beyond simply avoiding harmful chemicals; it involves prioritizing renewable resources, sourcing ingredients locally whenever feasible to reduce transportation emissions, and minimizing the use of water and energy in the manufacturing process. They have a detailed ingredient list and transparency about their sourcing which empowers customers to make informed choices that align with their values. This resonates particularly well with a growing consumer base that prioritizes ethical and environmentally conscious consumption. The shift in consumer preferences towards sustainability is not merely a trend; it reflects a fundamental change in values, creating a significant market opportunity for companies that genuinely embrace environmental responsibility.

Beyond ingredients, Seventh Generation's dedication to sustainability extends to its packaging. The company actively pursues minimizing packaging waste through innovative design and the use of recycled and recyclable materials. They actively advocate for reducing reliance on single-use plastics and actively explore biodegradable and compostable alternatives, frequently sharing their successes and challenges in their communication materials. This proactive transparency helps educate consumers about sustainable practices and builds trust, strengthening brand loyalty. The commitment extends to the post-consumer phase of the product life cycle. They actively participate in recycling programs and support initiatives aimed at reducing landfill waste. This comprehensive approach, encompassing the entire lifecycle of their products, sets them apart from companies whose sustainability efforts are limited to the manufacturing process alone.

The company's commitment transcends its internal operations; they actively engage in advocacy and collaborative efforts to promote broader environmental sustainability. This is not just about reducing their own impact but actively contributing to a larger systemic shift toward environmental responsibility. They participate in initiatives to promote sustainable agriculture, support policies that protect natural resources, and actively educate the public about environmental issues through various channels, including social media, educational materials, and collaborations with environmental organizations. This commitment demonstrates their belief that environmental sustainability is not merely a corporate responsibility, but a shared societal responsibility.

However, Seventh Generation's journey hasn't been without its challenges. Balancing environmental sustainability with economic viability has often required innovative approaches and creative solutions. Sourcing sustainable ingredients and eco-friendly packaging can sometimes lead to higher costs, requiring strategic pricing and marketing to remain competitive. Maintaining transparency and communicating their commitment authentically, especially when facing setbacks or unexpected challenges in their supply chain, requires consistent vigilance and thoughtful communication strategies. Their transparency, however, is key to building trust and loyalty. When faced with issues of sourcing or production, their openness has helped maintain customer confidence and even strengthen their brand reputation.

Another significant challenge arises from the complexity of global supply chains. Ensuring that sustainable practices are upheld throughout the entire supply chain, from raw material sourcing to final product distribution, requires meticulous monitoring and collaboration with suppliers. This necessitates robust verification processes and continuous improvements to their supply chain management systems. They openly acknowledge these challenges and proactively address them, maintaining transparency with their consumers. This commitment to honesty and accountability further solidifies their brand image.

Nevertheless, their dedication to sustainability is evident not only in their practices but also in their long-term success. Their focus on eco-friendly products has resonated strongly with environmentally conscious consumers, leading to significant brand loyalty and strong market share. They've demonstrated that environmental responsibility is not at odds with profitability but can be a powerful driver of both. This showcases the increasing market demand for sustainable and ethically produced goods. Their success helps inspire other businesses to adopt similar approaches, illustrating that a conscious business model is not only morally right but also financially viable.

Seventh Generation's commitment to environmental sustainability serves as a compelling case study for other businesses seeking to integrate conscious practices into their operations. Their journey underscores several key lessons: first, environmental sustainability needs to be integrated into every aspect of the business, from product design to supply chain management; second, transparency and open communication are essential to building trust and engaging consumers; and third, a commitment to sustainability requires consistent vigilance, ongoing innovation, and a willingness to address challenges proactively and transparently. Their success demonstrates the potential for businesses to thrive while making a positive impact on the environment, proving that ethical and sustainable practices aren't simply an idealistic aspiration, but a viable and potentially highly successful business model. The journey of Seventh Generation inspires other businesses to consider the far-reaching impact of their operations and embrace a more holistic approach to their responsibilities, shifting from a focus on short-term profits to a longer-term, more sustainable vision. Their efforts show that aligning business with environmental responsibility is not a sacrifice, but a journey towards a more resilient and successful future.

The impact of Seventh Generation extends beyond its direct operations. Their advocacy efforts, collaborations with environmental organizations, and public education initiatives have helped raise awareness about environmental issues and promote broader societal change. They've been instrumental in influencing industry standards and best practices, demonstrating the potential of a single company to influence the entire business landscape. Their commitment inspires not just consumers, but other businesses to rethink their approaches and adopt more sustainable practices. This demonstrates the potential for ripple effects: a company's commitment to environmental responsibility can trigger wider positive changes across the industry and society as a whole.

In conclusion, Seventh Generation's story highlights the transformative power of conscious business. Their unwavering dedication to environmental sustainability, combined with their transparent communication and proactive advocacy, has not only built a successful and loyal customer base, but also created a significant positive impact on the environment and the business world. They've convincingly demonstrated that environmental responsibility and business success are not mutually exclusive but can be mutually reinforced. Their journey serves as a powerful testament to the potential of businesses to be agents of positive change, inspiring a shift toward a more sustainable and equitable future for all. Their legacy continues to inspire and challenge other organizations to adopt more environmentally responsible practices, leaving a lasting impact on the business world and the planet. The ongoing evolution of their practices and their adaptation to the ever-changing environmental landscape will continue to provide valuable lessons for future generations of conscious leaders and entrepreneurs.

Reflection

4. Eight Case Studies of Conscious Businesses from Various Sectors

Beyond Patagonia, Unilever, and Seventh Generation's exemplary journeys, a diverse range of businesses are demonstrating the viability and profitability of conscious business practices. This section explores eight case studies, each illustrating the unique application of these principles across various sectors. These examples highlight the versatility and adaptability of conscious business, demonstrating that its principles are not limited to a single industry or niche market but are applicable across the spectrum of commercial activity.

1. In the realm of food and beverage, consider **Danone**'s commitment to sustainable agriculture and ethical sourcing. Danone's initiatives focus on supporting farmers and promoting biodiversity, reflecting a deeper understanding of the interconnectedness of their business with the environment and social wellbeing. Their investment in sustainable farming practices not only ensures the quality and availability of their raw materials but also contributes to the overall health of the planet. Danone actively publishes sustainability reports and engages in transparent communication, demonstrating a commitment to accountability and fostering trust with consumers. This approach strengthens their brand image and reinforces customer loyalty, highlighting the competitive advantage

of embracing sustainable and ethical practices in the long term. Their commitment extends to working with their suppliers to implement sustainable practices across their supply chain, demonstrating a holistic and integrated approach to sustainability.

2. The beauty industry offers another compelling example with **Lush Cosmetics**, which champions fair trade and ethical sourcing, avoiding animal testing and employing minimal packaging. Lush's unique approach to marketing, emphasizing customer interaction and community building, is integral to its conscious business model. Their success illustrates the importance of fostering a strong brand identity rooted in ethical values. The strong customer loyalty they cultivate stems from an emotional connection built on shared values and a belief in the company's mission. Their active involvement in environmental and social causes aligns their business with consumer values, thereby reinforcing brand loyalty and driving sales. The transparent nature of their ingredient sourcing and production processes, openly communicating about both successes and challenges, contributes to building trust and further strengthens their connection with customers.

3. Moving into the tech sector, we examine companies like **Salesforce**, known for their robust corporate social responsibility programs and their commitment to environmental stewardship. Their initiatives focus on sustainable practices in their own operations but also extend to empowering other companies and communities to embrace responsible practices. Their investment in sustainability technologies and their support for various social causes actively contribute to positive social and environmental impact. Salesforce's influence within the technology sector is significant, demonstrating the potential for large corporations to leverage their size and resources to drive positive change within their industry. Their focus on employee engagement, incorporating social responsibility

into their corporate culture, fosters a strong sense of shared purpose and enhances employee morale.
4. In the financial services sector, companies like **Triodos Bank** prioritize ethical lending practices and investing in businesses aligned with social and environmental values. This selective approach to investment demonstrates a clear alignment of financial goals with broader social and environmental considerations, showing a strong commitment to responsible capitalism. By meticulously selecting investments that align with their values, they demonstrate that financial success and social impact are not mutually exclusive. They challenge the traditional view of financial institutions, showcasing the potential for the financial sector to play a significant role in driving positive change and promoting a more sustainable and equitable future. The transparency of their investment policies and their clear communication of their ethical criteria builds trust and attracts customers who share similar values, showcasing the power of aligning business practices with consumer values.
5. The healthcare industry is represented by companies like **Honest Company**, a consumer goods company known for its commitment to safe and sustainable products for children. Their focus on transparency and safety standards directly reflects consumer values concerning the health and well-being of their families. The company's commitment to sustainable packaging and ethical sourcing demonstrates that a commitment to responsible business practices can coexist with innovation and market success. Their strong brand loyalty stems from customer trust and satisfaction, built on a foundation of transparency and a dedication to producing quality, safe, and sustainable products. The success of Honest Company demonstrates the significant market demand for ethical and sustainable consumer products, particularly in the sensitive area of children's products.

6. Another sector offering an example is the energy sector. Companies like **Enel Green Power** are focused on renewable energy sources, demonstrating that large-scale energy production can be achieved while minimizing environmental impact. Their commitment to sustainable energy solutions addresses a critical global challenge and showcases the potential for profitability within environmentally responsible practices. Their investments in renewable technologies demonstrate a proactive and forward-thinking approach to mitigating climate change, illustrating that sustainable practices are not simply a cost but a key driver of innovation and growth. Their success provides a model for other energy companies to transition towards a cleaner and more sustainable future.

7. Within the manufacturing industry, companies like **Interface**, a global flooring company, demonstrate the potential for significant environmental improvements through a commitment to sustainable manufacturing. Their commitment to minimizing their environmental footprint through innovations in materials and manufacturing processes demonstrate the ability to integrate environmental responsibility throughout the entire product life cycle. Their ongoing commitment to reducing waste, conserving energy, and minimizing their impact on the environment underscores a long-term commitment to sustainability. Their success highlights the possibility of balancing profitability with profound environmental stewardship. The company's ongoing commitment to transparent reporting and ongoing efforts to further reduce environmental impact showcases a continuous commitment to sustainable business practices.

8. Finally, in the retail sector, consider companies like **Whole Foods Market**, known for their commitment to organic and locally sourced products, showcasing the power of connecting with local communities and promoting ethical sourcing. Their commitment to working with local farmers

and producers strengthens their relationship with the community while upholding quality and sustainability standards. This collaborative approach builds trust and fosters a sense of community, differentiating them from larger, less locally focused retail chains. Their focus on sustainability and fair-trade practices resonates with consumers who value ethical sourcing and environmental responsibility. Their ongoing commitment to working with small-scale farmers and local suppliers demonstrates a commitment to sustainable and equitable business practices, showcasing the potential for retail businesses to actively contribute to the well-being of their communities.

These eight case studies illustrate the breadth and depth of conscious business practices across various industries. They demonstrate that incorporating social and environmental responsibility into business strategies is not only ethically sound but also a powerful driver of innovation, growth, and long-term success. Each case study offers unique lessons, highlighting the importance of adaptability, transparency, and a deep commitment to creating positive impact. Their combined success underscores the growing market demand for products and services from companies with a proven commitment to sustainability and ethical practices. The journey of these conscious businesses provides invaluable insights and inspiration for entrepreneurs and leaders seeking to build businesses that thrive while contributing to a more sustainable and equitable future for all.

Reflection

Chapter 9: The Future of Quantum Business

1. The Future of Conscious Capitalism

The examples presented thus far demonstrate the tangible impact of conscious business practices on individual companies and their stakeholders. However, the potential of conscious capitalism extends far beyond individual success stories; it offers a blueprint for a fundamentally different economic paradigm. This paradigm shift is driven by a growing awareness of the interconnectedness of business, society, and the environment. Consumers, investors, and employees are increasingly demanding transparency, ethical sourcing, and a commitment to social and environmental responsibility from the businesses they engage with. This evolving landscape presents both challenges and unprecedented opportunities for businesses willing to embrace a future defined by conscious capitalism.

One of the most significant trends shaping the future of conscious capitalism is the rise of stakeholder capitalism. Traditional models prioritize shareholder value above all else, often at the expense of employees, customers, communities, and the environment. However, a growing number of businesses are recognizing that long-term success depends on building strong relationships with all stakeholders. This involves creating a culture of collaboration and transparency, actively engaging stakeholders in decision-making processes, and measuring success not just in financial terms but also in terms of social and environmental impact. This shift necessitates a fundamental re-evaluation of corporate governance structures and performance metrics, demanding the integration of environmental, social, and governance (ESG) factors into core business strategies. Companies are increasingly adopting ESG reporting frameworks to provide stakeholders with a comprehensive view of their social and environmental performance. These reports aren't merely compliance exercises; they represent a commitment to transparency and accountability, fostering trust and strengthening relationships with investors and customers.

Another significant trend is the growing influence of technology in driving conscious business practices. Technology enables greater transparency and traceability throughout supply chains, allowing businesses to monitor and improve labor practices, environmental impact, and product sourcing. Blockchain technology, for instance, is being used to track the origin of goods, ensuring ethical and sustainable sourcing. Artificial intelligence (AI) and machine learning can help optimize resource allocation, reduce waste, and improve efficiency, minimizing the environmental footprint of business operations. Furthermore, data analytics tools empower companies to measure and report on their social and environmental impact with greater precision, providing insights that inform future strategic decisions and demonstrate the effectiveness of their conscious initiatives. The adoption of these technologies isn't simply about improving efficiency; it's about fundamentally changing how businesses operate, fostering a more responsible and sustainable approach to production and distribution.

The increasing awareness of climate change is another pivotal factor shaping the future of conscious capitalism. Businesses are under growing pressure to reduce their carbon emissions and adopt sustainable practices. This necessitates significant investments in renewable energy, energy-efficient technologies, and sustainable supply chain management. Companies are exploring innovative approaches to carbon offsetting and developing strategies to achieve net-zero emissions. However, addressing climate change requires more than simply reducing a company's own carbon footprint. Conscious businesses are also playing a leading role in advocating for climate-friendly policies and actively engaging in initiatives to promote climate action. This proactive engagement demonstrates a commitment to a broader societal responsibility, extending beyond internal operations to influence systemic change. The transition to a low-carbon economy is not just a regulatory imperative; it presents a significant opportunity for businesses to innovate and develop new products and services. The demand for sustainable alternatives is growing rapidly, creating new market niches and fostering entrepreneurial innovation.

The future of conscious capitalism also hinges on the growing demand for purpose-driven brands. Consumers are increasingly making purchasing decisions based on their values, choosing to support businesses that align with their social and environmental concerns. This creates a strong incentive for businesses to build a strong brand identity rooted in ethical values and a clear purpose beyond simply generating profits. This "purpose-driven" approach builds stronger customer loyalty, fosters stronger employee engagement, and attracts investors who are increasingly interested in supporting companies with a demonstrably positive social impact. However, authenticity is paramount; consumers are quick to identify "greenwashing" or superficial attempts to appear socially responsible. True purpose-driven businesses demonstrate a genuine commitment to their values, which is reflected in their operations, their supply chains, and their communication with stakeholders.

Furthermore, the growing influence of impact investing is fundamentally reshaping the financial landscape. Impact investors prioritize not only financial returns but also positive social and environmental impact. This approach is driving significant investments in conscious businesses, providing crucial capital for growth and expansion. Impact investing is not just about philanthropy; it represents a sophisticated approach to investing that recognizes the inextricable link between financial success and social progress. This shift is driving a re-evaluation of traditional financial models, highlighting the potential for businesses to create both profits and positive social and environmental change. Impact investors are increasingly demanding transparency and rigorous measurement of social and environmental impact, further driving the adoption of ESG reporting frameworks and other accountability mechanisms.

The increasing importance of employee well-being and engagement is another critical trend. Conscious businesses recognize that their employees are their most valuable asset. Creating a positive and supportive work environment is not just an ethical imperative; it's also a strategic necessity for attracting and retaining top talent. This involves fostering a culture of inclusivity, diversity, and equity, offering competitive salaries and benefits, and providing opportunities for professional development and growth. Employees are increasingly seeking purpose in their work, wanting to be part of something bigger than themselves. Conscious businesses cater to this desire by clearly articulating their values and mission and by providing employees with opportunities to contribute to a positive social or environmental impact. Engaged and motivated employees are more productive, creative, and loyal, contributing significantly to the long-term success of the business.

The future of conscious capitalism also necessitates a fundamental shift in leadership styles. Traditional, top-down management approaches are increasingly ineffective in the modern business environment. Conscious leadership emphasizes collaboration, empathy, and a commitment to serving all stakeholders. Leaders are expected to be transparent, accountable, and actively engage their employees in decision-making processes. They prioritize the well-being of their employees and foster a culture of trust and mutual respect. This shift in leadership is critical for building a sustainable and equitable business model that aligns with the evolving values and expectations of consumers, investors, and employees. Conscious leaders are not simply managers; they are stewards of their businesses, responsible for building sustainable and ethical organizations that contribute to the well-being of society and the environment.

In conclusion, the future of conscious capitalism is bright, but it requires a fundamental shift in mindset and business practices. The trends outlined above highlight the growing importance of stakeholder capitalism, technology, climate action, purpose-driven brands, impact investing, employee well-being, and conscious leadership. Businesses that embrace these trends are not only better positioned to succeed in the long term but are also playing a vital role in creating a more equitable, sustainable, and prosperous world.

The transition to conscious capitalism is not just about adopting a few new practices; it's about fundamentally reimagining the role of business in society, aligning profits with purpose and building a future where economic success and social progress are mutually reinforcing. The path ahead is challenging, but the potential rewards – both for individual businesses and for society as a whole – are immense. The time for conscious capitalism is not merely approaching; it is here, demanding action and innovation from businesses and leaders alike.

Reflection

2. A Call to Action Embracing the Quantum Leap

The journey we've undertaken together through these chapters has illuminated a path towards a profoundly different way of doing business – a way that transcends the limitations of outdated models and embraces the boundless potential of consciousness. We've explored the foundational principles of conscious business, delved into the critical role of regenerative practices, and examined the urgent need for a transformative shift in leadership development. But the true power of this knowledge lies not in its passive consumption, but in its active application. This is not a theoretical exercise; it's a call to action.

The shift to a conscious business model requires a quantum leap – a fundamental shift in perspective, values, and operating principles. It's about moving beyond the narrow confines of profit maximization to embrace a holistic vision that encompasses social justice, environmental stewardship, and the well-being of all stakeholders. This is not merely a matter of corporate social responsibility; it's a complete reimagining of the very purpose of business itself.

This transformation begins within. Before we can change the world, we must change ourselves. This means cultivating a heightened level of self-awareness, embracing ethical decision-making, and developing emotional intelligence to navigate the complexities of human interaction. It requires a commitment to continuous learning and a willingness to challenge our own biases and assumptions. Mindfulness practices, meditation, and other contemplative disciplines can significantly enhance this inner transformation, fostering greater clarity, compassion, and resilience.

The principles outlined throughout this book provide a roadmap for this inner journey. The cultivation of intentionality, the practice of presence, and the conscious engagement with our values form the bedrock of conscious leadership. By aligning our actions with our deepest values, we create a ripple effect that extends far beyond our immediate sphere of influence, creating a positive impact on our teams, our communities, and the world at large.

But inner transformation alone is insufficient. We must translate this inner work into tangible action within our organizations and the broader business landscape. This involves a concerted effort to integrate the principles of conscious business into every facet of our operations. It means re-evaluating our supply chains to ensure ethical sourcing and environmental sustainability, prioritizing employee well-being and fostering a culture of collaboration and empowerment. It means measuring our success not solely by financial metrics, but also by our social and environmental impact.

This requires a fundamental shift in how we define success. Traditional measures of profit and market share, while important, are insufficient indicators of true progress. We must broaden our metrics to include indicators of social and environmental responsibility, such as carbon footprint reduction, fair labor practices, community engagement, and ethical sourcing. By tracking and reporting on these indicators, we demonstrate our commitment to a holistic approach to business and hold ourselves accountable for our impact on the world.

The transition to a conscious business model also demands a fundamental re-evaluation of our leadership styles. Conscious leaders are not merely managers; they are stewards, visionaries, and catalysts for change. They prioritize collaboration over competition, empathy over dominance, and long-term sustainability over short-term gains. They empower their employees, fostering a culture of trust and mutual respect. They lead with integrity, transparency, and accountability.

This new breed of conscious leaders will require a different type of training and development. Traditional business schools, while providing valuable business acumen, often fall short in cultivating the ethical consciousness and holistic worldview needed to navigate the complexities of the 21st-century business landscape. A fundamental shift in business education is required, integrating ethics, sustainability, and social responsibility into the core curriculum. Experiential learning, case studies of successful conscious businesses, and mentorship opportunities from established conscious leaders are crucial components of this new educational paradigm.

Beyond formal education, lifelong learning is essential. Conscious leadership is not a destination; it's a journey of continuous growth and adaptation. Leaders must remain committed to expanding their knowledge, embracing new technologies and approaches, and adapting to the ever-evolving needs of a dynamic world. This includes actively seeking opportunities for networking and collaboration with other conscious leaders, sharing best practices, and fostering a sense of collective purpose.

Furthermore, the role of government and policy cannot be overlooked. Government incentives for sustainable business practices, ethical sourcing regulations, and support for educational initiatives focused on conscious leadership can create a more favorable environment for the growth of conscious businesses. Collaboration between businesses, governments, and educational institutions is critical to fostering a holistic ecosystem that supports the transition to a more sustainable and ethical business model.

The shift to a conscious business model is not merely a trend; it's a necessity. The challenges facing our planet – climate change, social inequality, and environmental degradation – demand a fundamental shift in our values and operating principles. Conscious business provides a framework for navigating these challenges, creating a more sustainable, equitable, and prosperous future for all. It's a future where profit and purpose are not mutually exclusive, but rather intertwined aspects of a thriving, regenerative economy.

This is a call to action for each of us. It's a call to integrate the principles of conscious business into our own lives and organizations, to lead with integrity, compassion, and a deep understanding of our interconnectedness. It's a call to embrace the quantum leap, to transcend the limitations of outdated models, and to create a future where business serves as a force for good in the world. The future of business, and indeed the planet, depends on it. Let us rise to the challenge and build a future worthy of our aspirations, a future where sustainability, ethics, and purpose converge to create a truly conscious and flourishing world.

The transition won't be easy. It will require courage, resilience, and a willingness to embrace uncertainty. There will be challenges, setbacks, and moments of doubt. But the potential rewards – a more just, equitable, and sustainable world – far outweigh the risks. The time for incremental change is over. We need a quantum leap, a fundamental shift in perspective and action. Are you ready to join the movement?

This is not just about creating a more sustainable business; it's about creating a more sustainable world. It's about building a future where profit and purpose are harmoniously integrated, where businesses are not just engines of economic growth, but also forces for positive social and environmental change. It's about cultivating a new generation of leaders who are not only competent and successful, but also compassionate, ethical, and deeply committed to making a positive impact on the world.

The journey ahead requires commitment, collaboration, and unwavering dedication. It requires a willingness to challenge the status quo, to question our assumptions, and to embrace a new paradigm of business that prioritizes people and the planet alongside profit. It demands a fundamental shift in our thinking, a re-evaluation of our values, and a commitment to continuous learning and growth.

This is not a task for a selected few; it's a responsibility for all of us. Businesses, leaders, entrepreneurs, and individuals all have a role to play in this transformative journey. By working together, embracing innovation, and prioritizing ethical and sustainable practices, we can create a world where business is a force for good, a catalyst for positive change, and a pathway to a brighter future for all.

The seeds of this transformation have been sown. Now, it's up to us to nurture them, to cultivate them, and to watch them grow into a flourishing, sustainable, and truly conscious future. The quantum leap awaits. Will you take it?

Reflection

3. Challenges and Future Prospects

Quantum business is an emerging field that integrates the principles of quantum mechanics into business operations, decision-making, and technological advancements. In this new reality, leadership is no longer solely about maximizing shareholder returns but about fostering sustainable, ethical, and adaptive organizations that can thrive amidst complexity. The digital revolution has dismantled conventional industry boundaries, forcing executives to rethink their competitive positioning, embrace ecosystem-based strategies, and cultivate agility at every level of their organizations. Furthermore, the widespread adoption of remote work, decentralized finance, and stakeholder capitalism demands a leadership approach that is fluid, interconnected, and values driven. This shift underscores the urgency of integrating conscious decision-making into corporate strategy, ensuring that businesses prioritize the well-being of all stakeholders rather than focusing solely on short-term profits.

In a world where corporate responsibility is no longer optional, businesses must evolve beyond outdated economic models that prioritize profit at the expense of people and the planet. The Quantum Business framework provides an opportunity to redefine capitalism through a lens of consciousness, ensuring that organizations operate in a manner that aligns financial success with ethical responsibility. This means moving from extractive business practices to regenerative models that foster long-term prosperity for all stakeholders, including employees, customers, investors, and the environment. Conscious Capitalism, as a foundational pillar of Quantum Business, recognizes that businesses are not isolated economic entities but active participants in a broader societal ecosystem. Companies that integrate conscious capitalism principles understand that profitability and purpose are not mutually exclusive—they are intrinsically linked. Organizations that uphold these principles cultivate strong, trust-based relationships with their stakeholders, resulting in higher employee engagement, brand loyalty, and long-term financial stability.

As we step into an era where global challenges such as climate change, economic inequality, and digital disruption demand urgent action, businesses must recognize that their survival depends on their ability to contribute positively to society. Leaders must shift from short-term financial engineering to long-term value creation, recognizing that corporate sustainability is not just about reducing environmental impact but also about fostering inclusive economies, advancing human potential, and driving ethical innovation.

The rise of the Information Age in the late 20th century introduced complexities that classical business models struggled to accommodate. Globalization, technological innovation, and increased access to information gave rise to fast-moving markets, decentralized operations, and heightened customer expectations. The internet enabled businesses to expand beyond local markets, but it also intensified competition and accelerated the rate of change, making rigid strategic planning models obsolete.

The early 21st century saw an unprecedented shift with the emergence of the Fourth Industrial Revolution—characterized by AI, blockchain, IoT, and quantum computing—which further disrupted the traditional principles of business management. Organizations faced a constant state of flux, requiring leaders to develop adaptive, systems-based thinking rather than adhering to outdated command-and-control leadership models. In response to these challenges, business thinking must evolve into a Quantum Business Framework. This new paradigm moves beyond classical economics and mechanistic management by emphasizing:

- Interconnectivity: Recognizing that businesses are part of an interdependent network of stakeholders, where changes in one part of the system impact the whole.
- Adaptability: Shifting from rigid, long-term planning to agile and iterative decision-making models that allow organizations to pivot in response to external forces.
- Non-Linear Growth: Moving beyond predictable, incremental growth patterns and embracing emergent innovation, exponential scalability, and disruptive thinking.
- Human-Centric Leadership: Moving away from pure financial metrics to consider stakeholder well-being, ethical governance, and corporate responsibility as critical factors for sustainable success.

As quantum physics revolutionized classical mechanics by proving that energy and matter behave unpredictably at the smallest scales, Quantum Business challenges the notion of stability and predictability in corporate leadership. The future of business success will be defined by leaders who can anticipate change, embrace uncertainty, and create strategic value through a holistic, interconnected approach.

Business models have undergone multiple transformations throughout history, reflecting shifts in societal values, economic structures, and technological advancements. Classical business thinking, rooted in the principles of industrial capitalism, prioritized efficiency, resource optimization, and hierarchical control. The early industrial age was characterized by centralized decision-making, rigid corporate structures, and economies of scale. While these models fostered growth and innovation during periods of stability, they lacked the flexibility to respond to dynamic and complex global challenges.

Traditional business decision-making often relied on short-term financial gain, cost-cutting measures, and shareholder primacy, without considering long-term social and environmental consequences. The focus was primarily on efficiency, predictability, and risk minimization, often at the cost of innovation and sustainable development. Decisions were made in isolation, with little regard for their broader impact on employees, communities, and ecosystems.

However, the limitations of these outdated decision-making models became glaringly apparent with the rapid digital transformation and globalization of the 21st century. The rise of interconnected markets, artificial intelligence, climate concerns, and social movements has forced organizations to rethink their approach. The previous era's linear thinking and mechanistic decision-making models are no longer adequate in an economy defined by complexity, uncertainty, and constant change.

The failures of past decision-making models have been evident in corporate scandals, financial crises, environmental disasters, and workforce disengagement. For example, the 2008 financial crisis was largely a result of short-term profit-seeking behaviors, unsustainable risk-taking, and the lack of accountability for long-term consequences. Similarly, businesses that have ignored environmental concerns have faced backlash, regulatory fines, and declining consumer trust.

Reflection

Chapter 10: Quantum Business for C-Suite Leaders

1. Quantum Architect: Designing the Future Through Quantum Principles

Quantum mechanics, the branch of physics that studies subatomic particles, challenges traditional, deterministic models of reality. Unlike classical physics, which operates on fixed laws and predictable outcomes, quantum mechanics reveals a world of uncertainty, interconnectedness, and multidimensional potential. This shift from a rigid, linear perspective to one that embraces multiple possibilities has profound implications for business strategy, leadership, and innovation.

Among the most transformative quantum concepts is superposition, where a quantum particle exists in multiple states simultaneously until observed. Unlike traditional computers, which operate in binary code (1s and 0s), quantum computers leverage qubits, enabling parallel computations. In business, this translates into superposition thinking—the ability to hold multiple potential futures, strategies, or solutions at once rather than committing prematurely to a single approach.

Similarly, quantum entanglement describes how two or more quantum particles become intrinsically linked, meaning a change in one instantaneously affects the other, regardless of distance. In a business context, this principle underscores the deep interconnectivity between markets, supply chains, stakeholders, and global economies. Leaders who understand entanglement recognize that decisions made in one area of an organization or industry create ripple effects far beyond their immediate context, making systemic awareness critical for long-term success.

Another key concept, quantum tunneling, allows particles to pass through barriers that classical physics would deem impassable. In business, this represents breakthrough innovation—discovering solutions that traditional methods would overlook. For instance, quantum-inspired optimization models enable hyper-efficient routing strategies in logistics, reducing costs and delivery times in ways classical systems cannot.

By integrating these quantum principles into business operations, leaders unlock a new paradigm of strategic thinking—one that embraces uncertainty, optimizes complexity, and leverages interconnectivity to drive innovation and resilience.

Superposition Thinking – Embracing Multiple Possibilities

Traditional business decision-making forces leaders into binary choices: profit vs. purpose, centralization vs. decentralization, innovation vs. risk management. This either-or thinking limits organizations, reducing their ability to adapt, evolve, and thrive in an uncertain world. Superposition thinking challenges these false dichotomies by allowing businesses to hold multiple possibilities open at once, ensuring they remain agile and prepared for a range of potential outcomes.

Instead of committing to a rigid five-year plan, leaders develop fluid strategies that allow multiple potential futures to coexist until the most viable path emerges. This fosters innovation, adaptability, and resilience, enabling organizations to pivot seamlessly in response to shifting market dynamics.

For example, Amazon's leadership under Jeff Bezos exemplifies superposition thinking in action. Instead of choosing between different business models, Amazon simultaneously developed multiple industries—e-commerce, cloud computing (AWS), AI-driven logistics, and physical retail. This multi-dimensional approach created a self-reinforcing ecosystem, where advancements in one area fueled innovation across the company.

Similarly, Tesla does not limit itself to just automobiles. By integrating electric vehicles, solar energy, AI-driven autonomy, and battery technology, it ensures adaptability across multiple industries. This approach avoids the limitations of a single market and creates a strategic advantage in shaping the future of energy and transportation.

Quantum Leadership: Moving Beyond Linear Models

As businesses transition into an era defined by complexity, interconnectivity, and rapid transformation, traditional leadership models are proving inadequate. The Quantum Leader understands that the future is not a fixed destination but a realm of multiple possibilities.

This shift in leadership requires moving beyond rigid structures and predefined paths, embracing instead fluid, non-linear progression. Quantum leadership is characterized by:

- Adaptive Strategy Development – Leaders design organizations that pivot dynamically, exploring multiple parallel opportunities rather than committing prematurely to a single approach.
- Harnessing Collective Intelligence – Recognizing that intelligence and creativity emerge from interconnected networks rather than being confined to individuals.
- Holistic Decision-Making – Viewing the organization as a living system, where choices impact not just the business but the broader ecosystem of stakeholders, communities, and global economies.

Entanglement in Business: The Power of Interconnected Systems

The concept of entanglement reinforces the idea that no business decision exists in isolation. Organizations today operate within deeply interconnected ecosystems, where changes in one part of the system trigger cascading effects elsewhere.

A prime example is supply chain management. Companies that prioritize short-term cost savings by outsourcing production to countries with lax environmental regulations often face long-term reputational and operational consequences. Nike's outsourcing controversy in the 1990s highlights this reality. While benefiting from lower production costs, the company faced global backlash due to sweatshop labor, child exploitation, and environmental degradation. Consumer protests and boycotts forced Nike to restructure its supply chain and adopt more ethical sourcing practices, proving that isolated decisions can have far-reaching effects.

Similarly, fast fashion brands like Zara and H&M have faced scrutiny for their reliance on unsustainable production practices, contributing to excessive waste and environmental damage. The 2013 Rana Plaza factory collapse in Bangladesh, which killed over 1,100 workers, was a stark reminder of the human and environmental cost of unchecked outsourcing. These examples illustrate how short-term profit-driven decisions can lead to long-term consequences, affecting consumer trust, investor confidence, and regulatory scrutiny.

Resonance and Coherence: The Future of Organizational Design

Quantum leadership reshapes how organizations are structured. Traditional hierarchical models, designed for stability and control, are being replaced by fluid, decentralized, and self-organizing systems.

This transformation is evident in:

- Decentralized Leadership Models – Companies shift from rigid, top-down management to networks of empowered teams that self-regulate and innovate autonomously.
- Aligned Decision-Making – Leaders cultivate organizational coherence, ensuring that purpose, values, and actions remain synchronized across all levels.
- Resonant Cultures – Instead of enforcing compliance through rigid policies, businesses foster cultural alignment, where employees, stakeholders, and leadership operate in harmony toward a shared vision.

Tesla, SpaceX, and other quantum-inspired organizations exemplify this decentralized, innovation-driven approach, leveraging interdisciplinary collaboration and non-linear growth models to stay ahead of disruption.

The Quantum Business paradigm represents more than a shift in leadership—it is a fundamental evolution in how businesses operate, adapt, and create value. By embracing superposition thinking, entanglement, and quantum-inspired decision-making, organizations can move beyond outdated industrial-era models and navigate uncertainty with confidence. As the world becomes increasingly complex and interconnected, leaders must transition from linear, deterministic thinking to dynamic, multidimensional strategy development. Businesses that fail to adapt will struggle, while those that harness quantum principles will redefine industries, create sustainable impact, and pioneer the future of global commerce.

The next era of business belongs to those who dare to think beyond the binary, embrace paradox, and lead with conscious awareness. The Quantum Architect—the leader of tomorrow—understands that success is not about controlling the future but about co-creating it. The question is no longer whether businesses should make this shift, but rather—who will lead in this new quantum economy? The time for transformation is now.

Quantum Ecosystem

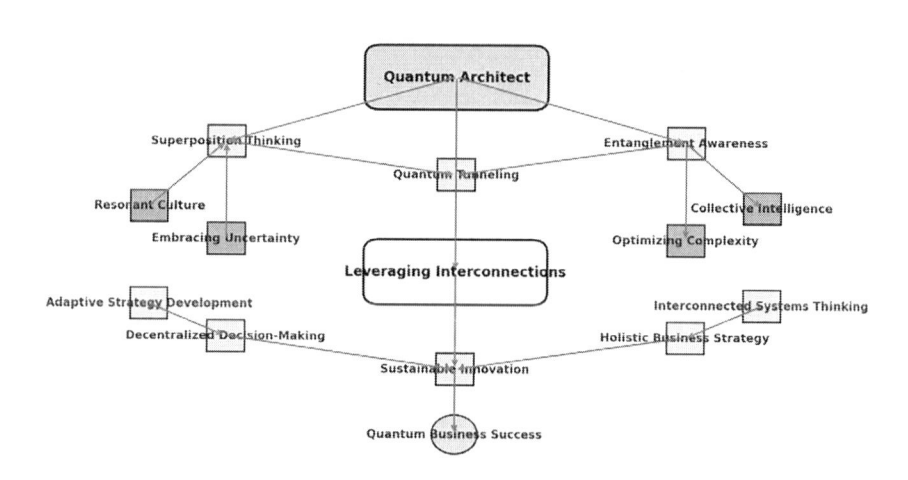

Reflection

2. Quantum Innovation: Redefining Creativity in a Quantum World

Innovation has long been the engine of progress, but in a world of increasing complexity, traditional innovation models struggle to keep pace with rapid change. Quantum Innovation leverages the principles of quantum mechanics—such as superposition, entanglement, and non-linearity—to unlock new dimensions of creativity, problem-solving, and transformation. This chapter explores the theoretical foundations of Quantum Innovation, its implications for leadership, and its ability to drive exponential breakthroughs in business and society.

Theoretical Foundations of Quantum Innovation

Quantum Superposition and Parallel Ideation

In quantum mechanics, superposition states that a particle can exist in multiple states at once until measured. This principle suggests that reality is not fixed but exists in a state of possibilities.

Quantum Innovation applies this concept to creativity, encouraging teams to hold multiple ideas simultaneously rather than prematurely selecting a single path. By maintaining multiple possibilities, organizations enhance their capacity for breakthrough innovations, fostering a mindset that welcomes ambiguity and divergence. In practical terms, businesses can benefit from running parallel innovation streams, allowing diverse solutions to co-evolve before choosing the most optimal direction.

Quantum Entanglement and Collective Creativity

Entanglement in physics describes how particles become deeply interconnected, influencing each other regardless of distance.

Quantum Innovation leverages this principle to highlight the interconnectedness of knowledge, skills, and perspectives across industries, disciplines, and individuals. Breakthroughs often emerge from seemingly unrelated fields colliding—an approach seen in industries like biotechnology, artificial intelligence, and sustainability. This interconnectedness allows for seamless knowledge transfer, driving synergies between disciplines that might otherwise remain siloed.

Quantum Tunneling and Disruptive Thinking

Quantum tunneling allows particles to move through energy barriers they would not traditionally surpass.

Applying this to innovation, organizations can "tunnel" past conventional constraints, whether technological, psychological, or structural. Quantum Tunneling suggests that with the right mindset and approach, perceived barriers are not absolute, leading to disruptive innovations that redefine industries. Companies that embrace quantum tunneling thinking remove restrictive mental models and policies, enabling exponential breakthroughs rather than linear progress.

Implications for Quantum Leadership in Innovation

Embracing Complexity and Non-Linearity

Traditional linear thinking is insufficient for navigating today's fast-paced world. Quantum leaders embrace complexity, leveraging non-linear thinking to explore new possibilities and solutions.

- **Systems Thinking:** Quantum leaders see the interconnectedness of business ecosystems, recognizing that small shifts can have significant ripple effects.
- **Adaptive Experimentation:** Rather than rigid strategies, organizations must embrace experimentation, rapid prototyping, and iteration, akin to the scientific method.
- **Complexity as an Asset:** Leaders who accept complexity as a fundamental reality develop more robust strategies that are adaptable to uncertainty.

Harnessing Collective Intelligence for Innovation

Quantum Innovation is not a solo act; it thrives in environments where knowledge is co-created and shared.

- **Open Innovation:** Quantum leaders cultivate ecosystems where employees, customers, and even competitors contribute to breakthroughs.
- **Cognitive Diversity:** Teams with varied perspectives, skills, and experiences generate richer and more disruptive solutions.
- **Quantum Leadership Networks:** Leaders must foster dynamic knowledge-sharing networks that enable collective intelligence to flourish.

Reshaping Organizational Culture for Innovation

To sustain Quantum Innovation, organizations must foster cultures of curiosity, agility, and bold experimentation.

- **Encouraging Risk-Taking:** Failure is not a setback but an essential component of the innovation process.

- **Quantum Agility:** Businesses must evolve rapidly, responding dynamically to emerging trends, technology, and market shifts.
- **Creating Safe Spaces for Experimentation:** Employees must feel psychologically safe to propose radical ideas and explore unconventional solutions.

Practical Applications of Quantum Innovation

Real-World Examples

- **Technology & AI:** Companies like OpenAI and Tesla leverage quantum-like thinking, fusing multiple fields to drive breakthroughs.
- **Healthcare:** Quantum Innovation in medicine has led to AI-assisted drug discovery and personalized treatments.
- **Sustainability:** Organizations integrating quantum-inspired solutions in energy and climate adaptation are redefining the future.

Implementing Quantum Innovation in Organizations

1. **Foster a Mindset of Exploration:** Encourage experimentation without the fear of failure.
2. **Break Down Silos:** Enable cross-disciplinary collaboration to drive novel insights.
3. **Embrace Emerging Technologies:** Stay at the forefront of AI, quantum computing, and biotech.
4. **Create an Innovation Ecosystem:** Cultivate partnerships with academia, startups, and research institutions.
5. **Develop Quantum-Resilient Strategies:** Adopt dynamic strategies that allow flexibility and rapid adaptation to shifting environments.

Conclusion

Quantum Innovation is not about incremental change but radical transformation. By embracing quantum principles, leaders can unlock new realms of possibility, positioning their organizations for sustained breakthroughs in a world that demands continuous reinvention. In an era defined by complexity, uncertainty, and rapid technological advancement, the capacity to think, create, and lead through a quantum lens is the key to designing the future. Quantum Innovators will not merely adapt to change; they will define it.

Reflection

3. Quantum Personal Excellence: A New Paradigm in Human Potential

In an era of rapid transformation and increasing complexity, traditional models of personal development often fall short of addressing the full potential of human consciousness. *Quantum Personal Excellence* integrates principles from quantum mechanics to redefine self-mastery, adaptability, and transformational leadership. This chapter explores the theoretical foundations of Quantum Personal Excellence, its implications for personal growth, and how individuals can cultivate resilience, creativity, and peak performance through a quantum approach to self-evolution.

Theoretical Foundations of Quantum Personal Excellence

Quantum Mechanics and Human Potential

Quantum mechanics, the study of matter and energy at its most fundamental level, challenges classical notions of determinism and linearity. These principles offer profound insights into personal excellence, revealing that growth is non-linear, interconnected, and influenced by conscious awareness.

Superposition and Infinite Possibilities

Superposition, a fundamental concept in quantum mechanics, suggests that particles exist in multiple states until observed or measured. This principle implies that individuals, too, exist within a realm of infinite potentialities, each awaiting activation through conscious choice and focused intention.

From a personal excellence perspective, this means that an individual is not bound by a single identity or capability. Instead, they can exist in multiple states of potential simultaneously, choosing which reality to actualize through mindset, decisions, and actions. This encourages a growth mindset where every challenge presents an opportunity to embody a new version of oneself.

Entanglement and Interconnectivity

Entanglement describes the quantum phenomenon where two particles, regardless of distance, become correlated such that the state of one instantaneously influences the other. This deep interconnectedness mirrors the human experience, where thoughts, emotions, and relationships are intricately linked.

Quantum Personal Excellence acknowledges that personal growth does not occur in isolation. Instead, individuals thrive within networks of influence, collaboration, and shared energy. By intentionally cultivating meaningful connections and aligning with high-frequency interactions, one can accelerate personal transformation and create ripple effects of excellence in wider communities.

The Observer Effect and Self-Perception

In quantum physics, the act of observation influences the behavior of particles. This phenomenon highlights the power of perception and conscious awareness. When applied to personal mastery, the observer effect suggests that how individuals perceive themselves directly impacts their abilities and potential. By shifting one's internal narrative from limitation to possibility, new pathways for growth and self-realization emerge. This principle underscores the importance of mindfulness, self-awareness, and intention in shaping one's destiny.

Implications for Quantum Leadership and Self-Mastery

Embracing Non-Linearity in Growth

Traditional models of personal development assume a linear progression—moving from one level of skill or awareness to the next in a predictable manner. However, Quantum Personal Excellence recognizes that growth is non-linear, occurring in quantum leaps rather than incremental steps.

- **Adaptive Resilience:** Rather than rigid goal setting, individuals must cultivate adaptability and openness to unforeseen possibilities.
- **Emergent Mastery:** Skill development occurs dynamically, often through breakthrough moments rather than gradual accumulation.

Harnessing the Power of Collective Intelligence

Personal excellence is amplified in collaborative, high-energy environments where knowledge, creativity, and inspiration flow freely.

- **Coherence with Like-Minded Individuals:** Just as quantum systems exhibit coherence, individuals who align with a collective purpose experience exponential growth.
- **Energy Synchronization:** Engaging in conscious collaboration enhances one's ability to access deeper insights and innovative thinking.

Expanding Conscious Awareness

Quantum principles emphasize that consciousness is fundamental to shaping reality. Individuals who cultivate heightened awareness can better navigate uncertainty and complexity.

- **Mindfulness and Intentionality:** Conscious decision-making enables individuals to create realities aligned with their highest aspirations.
- **Energetic Alignment:** Aligning personal energy with purpose-driven actions leads to deeper fulfillment and sustained success.

Practical Applications of Quantum Personal Excellence

Real-World Examples

- **Athletic Performance:** Elite athletes leverage mental conditioning techniques, visualization, and flow-state awareness, embodying the principles of quantum focus and peak potential.
- **Entrepreneurial Success:** Visionary leaders such as Elon Musk and Steve Jobs have demonstrated quantum-inspired thinking by integrating intuition, adaptability, and disruptive innovation into their work.
- **Holistic Well-Being:** Integrative health approaches that blend neuroscience, meditation, and bioenergetics reflect a quantum approach to personal wellness.

Implementing Quantum Personal Excellence in Daily Life

1. **Parallel Growth Strategies:** Engage in multiple areas of development simultaneously to unlock multidimensional potential.

2. **Cultivate Resonant Environments:** Surround yourself with people, spaces, and experiences that amplify your energy and inspire higher thinking.
3. **Practice Conscious Observation:** Be mindful of self-perception and intentionally shape your personal narrative toward empowerment.
4. **Embrace Quantum Leaps:** Recognize that transformation often happens suddenly, through paradigm shifts rather than slow progression.
5. **Develop an Adaptive Mindset:** Remain open to uncertainty, leveraging unexpected opportunities for accelerated growth.

Conclusion

Quantum Personal Excellence challenges the traditional paradigms of self-mastery by integrating quantum principles of interconnectedness, non-linearity, and conscious awareness. By embracing this approach, individuals unlock boundless potential, fostering personal evolution that is both dynamic and exponential. Through intention, mindfulness, and strategic energy alignment, Quantum Personal Excellence empowers individuals to not only reach peak performance but also create meaningful impact in their personal and professional spheres. As we continue to explore the limitless potential of human consciousness, this new paradigm offers a revolutionary pathway to self-actualization and collective transformation.

Reflection

4. Quantum Emotional Intelligence for C-Suite Leaders

The Evolution of Emotional Intelligence in Leadership

In the modern corporate ecosystem, the concept of emotional intelligence (EI) has evolved beyond conventional paradigms. It is no longer sufficient for C-suite leaders to merely understand and regulate their own emotions or empathize with others. The demands of a quantum business environment necessitate a multidimensional, non-linear approach—one that integrates the principles of quantum mechanics with the nuances of human emotion. This is what I call **Quantum Emotional Intelligence (QEI)**—a framework that aligns consciousness, intuition, and interconnectedness with strategic leadership.

Quantum Emotional Intelligence is a higher-order evolution of EI, leveraging the principles of quantum mechanics—superposition, entanglement, and uncertainty—to elevate leadership impact. In essence, QEI enables leaders to navigate complex business landscapes with an expanded awareness, fostering an organizational culture of agility, purpose, and sustainability.

Superposition: Holding Multiple Perspectives Simultaneously

In classical EI, leaders are trained to manage emotions and respond with composure. However, in a quantum business environment, decisions are rarely linear. The principle of superposition teaches us that multiple states exist at once until observed—much like the dynamic challenges faced by C-suite leaders who must balance paradoxes.

A QEI-driven leader does not see emotions and decisions in binary terms but instead acknowledges the coexistence of multiple emotional states and perspectives. They hold space for conflicting ideas, allowing for **simultaneous possibilities** rather than being confined to singular viewpoints. This ability to embrace complexity without prematurely collapsing possibilities into rigid decisions is what differentiates a quantum leader from a traditional one.

Entanglement: The Deep Interconnectedness of Leadership and Culture

Quantum entanglement suggests that two or more particles, once connected, remain linked regardless of distance. Similarly, in leadership, QEI acknowledges that emotional and energetic states within an organization are deeply intertwined. A leader's emotional state directly influences the collective consciousness of the company.

C-suite leaders who operate with QEI understand that their presence, words, and even unspoken emotions create ripple effects throughout their organization. They cultivate **intentional coherence**, ensuring that their emotional frequencies align with the company's mission and vision. This fosters psychological safety, employee engagement, and a culture of mutual trust.

The Uncertainty Principle: Navigating the Unknown with Emotional Agility

The Heisenberg Uncertainty Principle suggests that the more precisely we measure one property, the less precisely we can measure another. This applies directly to leadership in uncertain times. Business environments today are increasingly volatile, and the ability to predict outcomes with precision is an illusion.

QEI equips leaders with **emotional agility**, allowing them to remain centered in uncertainty rather than being reactive. Leaders who embody QEI are comfortable making decisions with incomplete information, trusting their intuitive intelligence as much as their analytical reasoning. They lead with **equanimity**, understanding that uncertainty is not a limitation but a space of creative potential.

Applying Quantum Emotional Intelligence in Leadership

For C-suite leaders to operationalize QEI, they must integrate three core practices into their leadership approach:

1. **Quantum Presence:** Cultivating deep self-awareness and presence in every interaction. Leaders must practice mindful leadership, ensuring that they are fully engaged in the moment rather than operating on autopilot.
2. **Resonant Decision-Making:** Utilizing both rational analysis and intuitive insight. Quantum leaders harmonize logic with deep inner knowing, making decisions that are not only strategic but also aligned with higher consciousness.
3. **Energetic Coherence:** Aligning personal emotional states with the energy they wish to cultivate in the organization. Leaders must regulate their emotional and energetic frequencies to inspire alignment within their teams.

The Future of Leadership: A Quantum Shift

Traditional emotional intelligence has served leaders well, but it is no longer sufficient for the complexities of the modern business landscape. The shift toward **Quantum Emotional Intelligence** represents an evolution in leadership consciousness, moving from control-based management to a more fluid, interconnected, and intuitive way of leading.

C-suite leaders who master QEI will not only future-proof their organizations but will also cultivate a workplace culture that is adaptive, purpose-driven, and deeply human. As we move into the quantum age of business, those who embrace this new paradigm will lead with greater authenticity, impact, and transformative influence.

The time to embrace Quantum Emotional Intelligence is now. The future of leadership depends on it.

Reflection

5. Quantum Communication Clarity for C-Suite Leaders

The Quantum Paradigm of Communication

In the fast-evolving landscape of business, the ability to communicate with absolute clarity has become an invaluable leadership trait. Yet, in an era defined by complexity, ambiguity, and rapid change, traditional communication models often fall short. To lead effectively, C-suite executives must adopt a **Quantum Communication Clarity (QCC)** approach—one that is multidimensional, dynamic, and attuned to the intricate interplay between language, perception, and energy.

Quantum physics has revealed that particles exist in multiple states simultaneously and that observation collapses possibilities into tangible reality. Similarly, communication in the quantum business realm is not a mere exchange of words but an interactive, co-creative process where clarity emerges from intentional awareness, deep resonance, and strategic alignment. By embracing the principles of **superposition, entanglement, and coherence**, leaders can cultivate a communication style that fosters trust, alignment, and exponential impact.

Superposition: The Power of Holding Multiple Realities

In classical communication, messages are often delivered in a linear, fixed manner. However, Quantum Communication Clarity recognizes that meaning is fluid and shaped by multiple perspectives. Just as quantum particles exist in multiple states until observed, leaders must acknowledge that every conversation contains multiple layers of meaning and interpretation.

C-suite leaders with QCC do not rush to impose singular interpretations. Instead, they hold space for multiple viewpoints, allowing dialogue to unfold dynamically before collapsing into a decision. This approach enhances problem-solving, fosters inclusivity, and ensures that communication aligns with the evolving nature of business realities.

Entanglement: The Interconnectedness of Words and Energy

Quantum entanglement suggests that particles remain connected regardless of distance. In communication, this translates to the profound impact that words, tone, and intent have on an organization's collective consciousness. Leaders who master QCC understand that their words are not isolated transactions; they are **energetic transmissions** that influence organizational culture, engagement, and trust.

To harness entanglement effectively, C-suite leaders must:

- Speak with **intentional precision**, ensuring that their messages are aligned with the organization's core values.
- Cultivate **empathetic resonance**, understanding that the emotional frequency behind their words is as crucial as the words themselves.
- Recognize the **non-local impact** of their communication, knowing that even a single statement can ripple through teams, stakeholders, and corporate ecosystems.

Coherence: Aligning Language with Purpose

In quantum physics, coherence refers to the harmonious alignment of particles that amplifies energy and stability. Likewise, communication that is coherent—aligned in purpose, clarity, and emotional intelligence—creates **organizational resonance** where teams and stakeholders move in unified momentum.

To achieve coherence in communication, leaders must:

1. **Calibrate Intentions:** Before speaking, they must align their words with their core mission and strategic vision.
2. **Ensure Clarity of Transmission:** Messages should be concise, precise, and unambiguous to prevent misinterpretation.
3. **Adapt to the Frequency of the Audience:** Leaders must recognize that different audiences operate at different cognitive and emotional frequencies, requiring nuanced approaches to engagement.

Practical Applications of Quantum Communication Clarity

To operationalize QCC in an executive leadership role, consider the following practices:

- **Quantum Listening:** Move beyond passive listening to fully engage with the speaker's words, intent, and underlying energy. Silence, patience, and presence become powerful tools in extracting deeper insights.
- **Strategic Pause:** Rather than reacting immediately, embrace the quantum principle of potentiality—pause to assess the full spectrum of possibilities before formulating a response.
- **Resonant Messaging:** Craft messages that are not only informative but also emotionally and energetically attuned to the audience, ensuring alignment and buy-in.

- **Feedback Loops:** Create iterative communication structures where feedback refines and enhances clarity rather than being seen as criticism.

The Future of Leadership: Quantum-Infused Communication

As the corporate landscape becomes increasingly complex, C-suite leaders who embrace Quantum Communication Clarity will differentiate themselves as visionary communicators capable of influencing change at both strategic and human levels. This is no longer just about delivering a message; it is about shaping reality through the **conscious orchestration of language, intention, and energetic alignment**.

By integrating the principles of quantum mechanics into their communication approach, leaders can cultivate deeper trust, alignment, and organizational agility. Quantum clarity is the new currency of leadership effectiveness. In this new era of business, those who master QCC will not only drive transformation but also inspire a new paradigm of conscious leadership.

The future of business communication is quantum. The time to embrace this shift is now.

Reflection

6. The Quantum Intuition Engine for C-Suite Leaders

In the ever-evolving landscape of global business, C-suite leaders must operate in an environment where uncertainty, complexity, and rapid transformation are the norm. Traditional decision-making frameworks, grounded in linear logic and historical data, are no longer sufficient. To thrive in the quantum era, leaders must harness an advanced cognitive and energetic capability—the **Quantum Intuition Engine (QIE)**—a multidimensional approach that integrates intuitive intelligence, quantum principles, and strategic foresight.

Quantum Intuition transcends mere instinct. It is a refined, dynamic process where leaders leverage superposition thinking, entanglement awareness, and quantum coherence to make real-time, high-impact decisions. This chapter explores the mechanics of QIE and how it enables C-suite executives to drive sustainable innovation, navigate ambiguity, and lead with unparalleled clarity.

The Quantum Nature of Intuition: A New Paradigm

Quantum mechanics has revealed that reality is not fixed but exists in a field of infinite possibilities until observed. Similarly, decision-making is not about selecting a single predetermined path but about **activating potentiality** through conscious intention. QIE enables leaders to operate in this non-linear space, where intuition is both a guiding force and a strategic tool.

Three key quantum principles inform the Quantum Intuition Engine:

1. **Superposition Thinking:** Leaders must hold multiple potential outcomes in their awareness simultaneously without prematurely collapsing into a single choice. This ability to embrace paradoxes and navigate uncertainty is the hallmark of a quantum leader.
2. **Entanglement Awareness:** Every decision, thought, and action is interconnected. Leaders who develop QIE recognize that their energy, words, and choices ripple across the organization and beyond, influencing stakeholders and markets in ways both seen and unseen.
3. **Quantum Coherence:** By aligning their internal emotional, mental, and energetic states, leaders can create coherence between their intuitive insights and external actions, fostering a leadership presence that is both decisive and adaptive.

Developing the Quantum Intuition Engine

QIE is not an abstract concept but a cultivated leadership skill. The following practices help leaders refine their quantum intuition and integrate it into high-stakes decision-making:

1. **Conscious Observation & Reflection**
    - Engage in daily reflective practices to heighten awareness of intuitive insights.
    - Use meditation, visualization, or mindfulness techniques to attune to subtle patterns and signals.
    - Journal intuitive nudges and track how they correlate with business outcomes.
2. **Energetic Sensory Perception**
    - Train yourself to sense the energy behind conversations, market trends, and emerging shifts.

- Develop a heightened ability to read non-verbal cues and emotional undercurrents in meetings.
- Trust the 'felt sense' of a decision before rationalizing it.

3. **Superposition Decision-Making**
   - Resist the urge for premature closure; instead, allow multiple strategic possibilities to coexist.
   - Utilize scenario mapping, where decisions are framed within multi-layered future trajectories.
   - Balance analytical data with intuitive data streams to form holistic solutions.

4. **Quantum Leadership Presence**
   - Cultivate an energetic frequency of clarity, confidence, and calm decisiveness.
   - Influence organizational culture by embodying a state of quantum coherence in decision-making.
   - Lead from a space of interconnected wisdom, recognizing the vast networks of potentiality at play.

Case Studies: Quantum Intuition in Action

Several pioneering business leaders and visionaries have demonstrated QIE in action, often making industry-defining decisions that defied conventional logic but proved profoundly effective.

- **Steve Jobs**: Renowned for his uncanny ability to foresee consumer trends before they materialized, Jobs operated with a deep reliance on intuitive intelligence, aligning innovation with emergent human desires.
- **Elon Musk**: His ventures into space travel and AI-driven technology reflect a capacity to act on intuitive foresight, often investing in markets that traditional analyst dismissed as implausible.
- **Indra Nooyi**: As CEO of PepsiCo, she integrated a systems-thinking approach, making strategic moves that balanced intuitive awareness with sustainable corporate growth.

These leaders exemplify how quantum intuition is not an esoteric concept but a pragmatic leadership advantage.

Integrating Quantum Intuition into Corporate Strategy

To systematize QIE within an organization, C-suite leaders must embed it into corporate strategy, fostering an environment where intuition is valued as a strategic asset rather than dismissed as subjective speculation.

1. **Cultural Adoption of Intuitive Leadership**
   - Encourage leadership teams to integrate reflective and intuitive methodologies in decision-making.
   - Create forums where intuitive insights are discussed alongside data-driven analysis.
2. **Training and Development Programs**
   - Implement executive coaching that enhances quantum intuitive capabilities.
   - Offer workshops that explore the integration of neuroscience, mindfulness, and quantum principles in leadership.
3. **Metrics of Quantum Decision Success**
   - Develop qualitative and quantitative indicators to assess the impact of intuition-driven decisions.
   - Evaluate correlation between intuitive decision-making and organizational agility, resilience, and profitability.

The Future of Leadership: Embracing Quantum Intuition

The corporate world is shifting toward a new leadership paradigm—one that demands agility, foresight, and a profound ability to navigate uncertainty. The Quantum Intuition Engine is not just a skillset; it is an essential competency for C-suite executives who seek to transcend outdated models of decision-making and enter the quantum era of business.

By embracing the principles of quantum mechanics in leadership, executives can refine their intuitive intelligence, synchronize with the energetic flow of innovation, and lead with greater vision and impact. The future belongs to those who harness the power of Quantum Intuition.

Now is the time to activate your Quantum Intuition Engine and lead with the wisdom, clarity, and foresight required to shape the next evolution of business.

Reflection

7. Quantum Energy Management and Resilience for C-Suite Leaders

In an era where leadership demands are intensifying, C-suite executives face unprecedented pressures that test their endurance, decision-making capabilities, and personal well-being. Traditional models of energy management focus on time optimization and physical stamina. However, in the quantum paradigm, energy is multidimensional—encompassing physical, mental, emotional, and spiritual dimensions. Leaders who master **Quantum Energy Management (QEM)** develop a resilient core, capable of sustaining high performance while fostering a culture of well-being within their organizations.

Quantum mechanics teaches us that energy is both a particle and a wave, fluctuating between states depending on observation and intention. Similarly, leadership energy is not a fixed resource but a dynamic field that can be expanded, directed, and renewed through conscious practices. Quantum Resilience, then, is the ability to remain centered and effective amidst turbulence, leveraging quantum principles such as **superposition, entanglement, and coherence** to maintain balance and drive impact.

Superposition: Holding Multiple States of Energy

In classical leadership, energy is often seen as a finite commodity—expended through effort and replenished through rest. However, quantum leadership recognizes that leaders can exist in multiple energy states simultaneously. A CEO can experience stress and confidence, urgency and calmness, fatigue and inspiration—all at once.

By cultivating **Quantum Superposition Thinking**, leaders learn to:

1. **Expand energy perception** – Recognizing that emotions and energy states are not binary but fluid and coexisting.
2. **Master emotional duality** – Embracing seemingly contradictory emotions and using them as fuel for strategic insight.
3. **Shift awareness proactively** – Choosing the most effective energetic state for any given situation rather than being trapped in reactionary cycles.

Leaders who practice this form of energy awareness can maintain high-performance levels without depleting themselves, accessing creativity even in high-stress environments.

Entanglement: The Energy Interconnectivity of Leadership

Quantum entanglement suggests that two particles, once connected, remain intertwined regardless of distance. This principle is deeply applicable to leadership energy: a leader's energetic state has profound effects on their teams, culture, and even external stakeholders.

Entanglement Awareness in leadership includes:

- **Recognizing energy transmission** – Understanding that personal stress, enthusiasm, or vision ripples through an organization.
- **Creating coherence in teams** – Aligning leadership energy with team purpose to create a synergistic work culture.
- **Developing energetic congruence** – Ensuring that words, actions, and emotional states are in harmony, fostering trust and stability.

When leaders become intentional about the energy they emit, they cultivate an organizational environment that fosters resilience, psychological safety, and sustained motivation.

Coherence: Synchronizing Leadership Energy for Resilience

Quantum coherence occurs when waves align, creating amplified power and stability. In leadership, coherence means aligning personal energy with vision, values, and actions, reducing internal friction and maximizing impact.

To cultivate **Quantum Coherence**, C-suite leaders must:

1. **Align daily practices with purpose** – Energy is wasted when actions do not align with core mission and values.
2. **Engage in high-frequency states** – Activities such as meditation, deep focus, and strategic solitude enhance clarity and energetic stability.
3. **Remove energetic distortions** – Identifying and eliminating activities, habits, or relationships that create energy leaks.

A coherent leader operates with clarity, resilience, and influence, fostering an environment where teams also function with synergy and focus.

Practical Strategies for Quantum Energy Management

To implement QEM, leaders must integrate both scientific and intuitive approaches to energy renewal and resilience:

1. **Morning Quantum Priming:**
   - Start the day with intentional energy setting (e.g., breathwork, visualization, or gratitude practices).
   - Align energy with strategic priorities rather than reactive urgency.
2. **Energetic Pulse Checks:**
   - Throughout the day, assess personal energy states and recalibrate if necessary.

- Shift states through music, movement, or focused breathing when energy dips.
3. **Quantum Recovery Cycles:**
   - Leverage ultradian rhythms by alternating intense focus with intentional recovery breaks.
   - Engage in nature, silence, or creative activities to restore mental and emotional energy.
4. **Resonant Leadership Influence:**
   - Set the energetic tone in meetings by consciously embodying clarity and presence.
   - Use language that amplifies possibility rather than reinforcing limitations.
   - Foster team resilience by guiding energy shifts through coaching and positive reinforcement.

The Future of Leadership: Energy Intelligence and Quantum Resilience

The leadership of the future will not be defined solely by intellect or strategy but by energy intelligence. Leaders who cultivate **Quantum Energy Management and Resilience** will drive impact not through force, but through mastery of their own vibrational frequency and the ability to create coherence in their organizations.

As businesses move deeper into the quantum age, resilience will no longer be about merely 'bouncing back' from adversity. Instead, it will be about **quantum adaptability**—the ability to **fluidly shift states, maintain energetic alignment, and amplify leadership presence** even in times of crisis.

The time to embrace this quantum shift is now. The future of leadership is energetic, intentional, and resilient. Are you ready to elevate your leadership energy to the next quantum level?

Reflection

8. Quantum Conscious Capitalism and Sustainability for C-Suite Leaders

In the age of rapid transformation and systemic complexity, business leaders are being called to evolve beyond traditional economic models toward a higher paradigm—**Quantum Conscious Capitalism**. This model integrates quantum principles with sustainable business practices, creating a multidimensional approach that fosters economic prosperity, social well-being, and environmental stewardship.

Traditional capitalism has often been defined by linear growth, profit maximization, and shareholder value. However, in a quantum reality, business success is non-linear, interconnected, and deeply influenced by energy, consciousness, and intention. **Quantum Conscious Capitalism (QCC)** challenges leaders to transcend old paradigms, embracing a more fluid and holistic approach that aligns profitability with planetary and human flourishing.

The Quantum Principles of Conscious Capitalism

Quantum physics has illuminated fundamental principles that parallel the evolution of sustainable business practices. These principles—**superposition, entanglement, and coherence**—offer profound insights for C-suite leaders seeking to integrate purpose, innovation, and long-term impact into their corporate strategies.

1. **Superposition: Holding Profit and Purpose Simultaneously**
    - Traditional business models often force a choice between profit and purpose. Quantum superposition reveals that both can exist simultaneously.
    - C-suite leaders must adopt a **dual-vision approach**, making strategic decisions that ensure financial viability while embedding social and environmental impact.
    - This shift requires new KPIs that measure value creation beyond financial returns—metrics that include stakeholder well-being, ecosystem health, and regenerative business practices.
2. **Entanglement: The Interconnectivity of Business and Society**
    - Just as quantum particles remain interconnected regardless of distance, businesses are deeply entangled with societal and environmental ecosystems.
    - Leaders who recognize this **interconnectivity** understand that their decisions ripple beyond the corporate walls, influencing communities, economies, and global systems.
    - The QCC mindset fosters **stakeholder capitalism**, where success is measured not only by shareholder returns but by the well-being of employees, customers, suppliers, and the planet.
3. **Coherence: Aligning Leadership Energy with Sustainable Outcomes**
    - In quantum mechanics, coherence refers to a state of energetic alignment that amplifies stability and impact.
    - For businesses, coherence emerges when corporate purpose, values, and operations are in harmony, creating a culture of trust, resilience, and innovation.

- Leaders must **embody coherence** by aligning personal integrity with corporate strategy, ensuring that sustainability initiatives are deeply integrated rather than performative.

Reflection

9. The Quantum Approach to Sustainable Business Practices

The transition to **Quantum Conscious Capitalism** requires practical strategies that embed sustainability at the core of business models. C-suite leaders can leverage quantum insights to drive systemic change in the following ways:

1. **Regenerative Business Models**
   - Moving beyond "sustainability" to **regenerative business**—where companies actively restore and enhance the environment rather than merely reducing harm.
   - Investing in **circular economy** initiatives that minimize waste, optimize resources, and create closed-loop systems.
   - Partnering with industries and stakeholders that prioritize biodiversity, ethical supply chains, and renewable energy.
2. **Energetic Leadership and Decision-Making**
   - Shifting from ego-driven, scarcity-based leadership to **quantum leadership**, where intuition, collaboration, and adaptability guide decision-making.
   - Practicing **energetic resilience**, ensuring that corporate leaders operate from a state of clarity and purpose rather than reactive urgency.

- Encouraging leadership teams to engage in mindfulness practices, deep listening, and systems thinking for holistic decision-making.
3. **Stakeholder Synchronization and Collective Intelligence**
   - Applying quantum entanglement to **stakeholder engagement**, ensuring seamless collaboration between employees, customers, investors, and policymakers.
   - Embracing **distributed leadership** models that leverage the collective intelligence of diverse perspectives rather than relying on hierarchical authority.
   - Creating **business ecosystems** that are adaptable, co-creative, and mutually beneficial rather than extractive and competitive.

The Future of Business: A Quantum Conscious Economy

The shift to Quantum Conscious Capitalism is not merely an ethical choice—it is a strategic imperative for long-term business resilience. As climate change, economic disparity, and technological disruptions accelerate, companies that **fail to adapt to quantum-conscious models will struggle to remain relevant**.
Leaders who embrace **quantum sustainability** will:

- Attract purpose-driven talent and conscious consumers who demand ethical business practices.
- Strengthen brand loyalty and investor confidence by demonstrating authentic commitment to planetary well-being.
- Future-proof their organizations by embedding **regenerative economics** and **impact-driven innovation** into their DNA.

The age of Quantum Conscious Capitalism is here. The question is not whether businesses will adapt, but how swiftly leaders will embrace the quantum shift and take responsibility for shaping a sustainable future. **Are you ready to lead the transformation?**

Reflection

10. Quantum Strategic Foresight and Scenario Planning for C-Suite Leaders

In the rapidly evolving business landscape, uncertainty and complexity have become the new constants. Traditional strategic planning, based on linear projections and historical data, is insufficient to navigate the multifaceted challenges of the quantum era. To thrive in this environment, C-suite leaders must embrace **Quantum Strategic Foresight**, a paradigm that integrates quantum principles—superposition, entanglement, and uncertainty—with advanced scenario planning methodologies.

Quantum Strategic Foresight enables leaders to perceive multiple possible futures simultaneously, adapt to shifting probabilities, and make agile, informed decisions in real time. This approach is not about predicting the future but about expanding the field of possibilities and positioning organizations to thrive in an interconnected, rapidly changing world.

Superposition Thinking: Holding Multiple Futures at Once

In classical strategy, organizations often plan for a single, probable future based on linear trends. However, the principle of superposition in quantum mechanics suggests that multiple futures exist simultaneously until observed or acted upon.

For leaders, this means:

1. **Developing Parallel Strategies** – Instead of committing to a single forecast, organizations must prepare for multiple plausible futures.
2. **Expanding Decision Horizons** – Leaders must cultivate the ability to hold seemingly contradictory possibilities without prematurely collapsing into one.
3. **Scenario Layering** – Constructing diverse and overlapping scenarios to anticipate market, geopolitical, technological, and social shifts.

By mastering superposition thinking, C-suite executives cultivate strategic flexibility and resilience, ensuring their organizations remain adaptable in times of uncertainty.

Quantum Entanglement: The Interconnectedness of Strategic Forces

Quantum entanglement suggests that once connected, particles remain linked regardless of distance. In the business world, seemingly unrelated factors—technological advancements, economic shifts, climate change, geopolitical events—are deeply entangled, influencing one another in unpredictable ways.

For Quantum Strategic Foresight, leaders must:

1. **Map Interdependencies** – Recognizing that business, society, and ecosystems are intricately connected, and small shifts in one domain can create cascading effects.
2. **Engage in Cross-Sector Intelligence** – Breaking down silos to gather insights from diverse industries, disciplines, and global perspectives.
3. **Leverage Networked Thinking** – Collaborating with ecosystems of partners, policymakers, and thought leaders to detect weak signals of change before they become disruptive forces.

When leaders acknowledge and leverage entanglement, they can anticipate ripple effects across industries, gaining a competitive edge in scenario planning.

The Uncertainty Principle: Embracing Probabilistic Decision-Making

The Heisenberg Uncertainty Principle states that we cannot simultaneously know both the position and momentum of a quantum particle. In business, this translates to the impossibility of predicting exact outcomes while still maintaining the ability to act strategically.

For effective scenario planning, leaders should:

1. **Adopt Probabilistic Thinking** – Recognizing that the future is composed of probability fields rather than fixed trajectories.
2. **Shift from Risk Aversion to Risk Adaptation** – Instead of avoiding uncertainty, leaders should build strategies that thrive in ambiguity.
3. **Develop Strategic Agility** – Creating frameworks that allow for rapid course correction as new information emerges.

By accepting uncertainty as an inherent part of strategic planning, executives move from rigid forecasting to dynamic positioning, enabling their organizations to pivot effectively in real-time.

Quantum Scenario Planning: A New Framework for Future Readiness

Traditional scenario planning involves constructing narratives around best-case, worst-case, and likely-case futures. Quantum Scenario Planning, however, expands this model by integrating multiple parallel realities, deep interconnectivity, and an openness to emergent possibilities.

Steps to Implement Quantum Scenario Planning:

1. **Identify Quantum Drivers of Change** – Recognizing macro and micro forces that influence future landscapes, including technology, environment, social shifts, and geopolitical tensions.
2. **Develop Multidimensional Scenarios** – Constructing narratives that include not only economic and operational variables but also human consciousness, collective behavior, and technological singularities.
3. **Run Superposition Simulations** – Instead of a single strategy, testing multiple strategic responses simultaneously through AI-driven modeling, cross-industry think tanks, and experimental pilots.
4. **Leverage Quantum Decision Trees** – Developing adaptable decision trees that allow for real-time scenario evolution as new data emerges.
5. **Practice Scenario Awareness** – Training leadership teams to recognize patterns and signals of change that indicate shifts toward one scenario or another.

This approach ensures that leaders are not reacting to change but are actively shaping and co-creating future realities.

The Future of Strategic Leadership: Quantum Readiness

Quantum Strategic Foresight and Scenario Planning are not just tools; they represent a new way of thinking about the future. As businesses transition into a quantum-driven world, those who embrace **quantum agility, interconnected vision, and multidimensional foresight** will lead industries forward.

C-suite executives who adopt Quantum Strategic Foresight will:

- Shift from **predictive forecasting** to **adaptive future sensing**.

- Develop **organizations that thrive in uncertainty** rather than resist it.
- Leverage **quantum intelligence to navigate disruptions** with clarity and precision.

The question is no longer whether leaders should integrate quantum principles into strategy but how quickly they can do so to maintain a competitive advantage. The future is not fixed—it is an evolving field of potentiality waiting for conscious leaders to shape it.

Are you ready to step into the quantum era of strategic leadership?

Reflection

11. Quantum Wealth and Value Creation for C-Suite Leaders

The traditional paradigms of wealth creation are rooted in linear, mechanistic models of growth—accumulation, extraction, and scarcity-driven competition. However, as we transition into an era defined by **Quantum Business**, it becomes imperative for C-suite leaders to shift their perspective on wealth, prosperity, and value creation. **Quantum Wealth** is not merely financial; it is an expansive, multidimensional construct that incorporates consciousness, energy, and interconnectivity. It aligns with the principles of **Quantum Economics**, which emphasize non-linearity, potentiality, and infinite value generation.

Unlike conventional economics, which assumes a zero-sum game, **Quantum Wealth Creation** acknowledges that value is infinite and can be generated without depletion. Through **quantum entanglement, superposition, and coherence**, leaders can reimagine wealth as a dynamic, ever-expanding ecosystem where financial, human, social, and planetary capital coexist in harmony.

Superposition: The Infinite Possibilities of Wealth

In classical business models, wealth is often viewed in binary terms—profit vs. loss, success vs. failure. However, quantum mechanics teaches us that multiple states can exist simultaneously until an observer collapses them into reality. This concept of

superposition provides a powerful lens for C-suite leaders to approach value creation.

Key Insights for Leaders:

1. **Expanding Wealth Beyond Profit** – Organizations must recognize that wealth encompasses **intellectual capital, emotional well-being, social impact, and regenerative economic models.**
2. **Multi-Dimensional Value Creation** – Businesses can operate in multiple value states at once—**generating profit while fostering sustainability, advancing technology while prioritizing ethics, and scaling operations while preserving organizational culture.**
3. **Quantum Decision-Making** – Leaders must hold multiple potential outcomes simultaneously, making choices that optimize both short-term gains and long-term legacy.

By embracing the principle of superposition, C-suite executives can craft organizations that are resilient, adaptive, and capable of generating **continuous, non-linear wealth.**

Entanglement: The Interconnected Wealth Ecosystem

Quantum entanglement demonstrates that two particles, once connected, remain intertwined regardless of distance. In the realm of business, this principle underscores the **deep interconnectivity between financial success, stakeholder well-being, and planetary health.**

Strategies for Leaders:

1. **Stakeholder Capitalism as a Quantum System** – Organizations must shift from an isolated shareholder-centric approach to **an entangled stakeholder ecosystem**, ensuring that financial prosperity is inextricably linked

to employee well-being, customer empowerment, and societal progress.
2. **Quantum Wealth Networks** – Wealth is no longer an isolated metric but a **relational and energetic force** that expands through networks of collaboration, co-creation, and shared purpose.
3. **Holistic Impact Measurement** – Organizations should integrate **quantum-informed impact metrics**, assessing value through financial, ecological, and human-centric KPIs.

Entanglement in wealth creation ensures that prosperity is not confined to the corporate balance sheet but radiates across industries, societies, and ecosystems, **maximizing holistic abundance.**

Coherence: Aligning Energy and Purpose for Exponential Growth

Quantum coherence occurs when waves align harmoniously, amplifying energy and stability. In business, coherence manifests when **organizational mission, leadership values, and operational strategies are in complete alignment.**

Coherence-Driven Wealth Strategies:

1. **Purpose-Driven Prosperity** – Wealth creation must be **aligned with organizational purpose**, ensuring that financial gains are a byproduct of meaningful impact.
2. **Energy-Optimized Leadership** – C-suite leaders must cultivate energetic coherence through **mindful leadership, conscious decision-making, and purpose-aligned execution.**
3. **Resonant Business Models** – Companies should design **quantum-coherent value chains**, ensuring that suppliers,

investors, employees, and customers are energetically aligned toward a **shared vision of prosperity.**

When organizations achieve quantum coherence, they enter a state of **exponential wealth creation**, where growth is not forced but emerges effortlessly from aligned action and strategic resonance.

The Quantum Paradigm of Infinite Value

Quantum Wealth Creation does not conform to scarcity-based thinking but instead embraces **abundance, expansion, and flow**. The old paradigms of competition and market domination are being replaced by **collaboration, regenerative economics, and conscious wealth distribution**.

How Leaders Can Activate Infinite Value:

1. **Quantum Reciprocity** – Wealth circulates in dynamic energy exchanges. Leaders must create systems where **giving and receiving** are balanced, ensuring sustainable and ethical economic models.
2. **Scaling Conscious Wealth** – Businesses must **scale impact before scaling profit**, ensuring that their expansion **uplifts communities, safeguards resources, and enriches human potential**.
3. **Transcending Linear Value Chains** – By leveraging **quantum supply webs**, organizations can create multi-directional, **adaptive** economic structures that flow with market changes rather than resisting them.

Conclusion: The Future of Wealth in the Quantum Age

As business transitions into the quantum era, **C-suite leaders must move beyond outdated wealth paradigms** and embrace the **limitless potential of Quantum Value Creation**. Financial capital will no longer be the sole determinant of success; instead, organizations that master **superposition (expanding possibilities), entanglement (deep connectivity), and coherence (energetic alignment)** will shape the future of prosperity.

The **new wealth equation** is not simply about increasing revenue; it is about **expanding consciousness, creating regenerative impact, and orchestrating a reality where success is infinite, multidimensional, and purpose driven**.

The shift to **Quantum Wealth Creation is not optional**—it is an evolutionary imperative. The leaders who master this paradigm will not only future-proof their organizations but will **define the next generation of global prosperity**.

Are you ready to embrace the **Quantum Future of Wealth**?

Reflection

Conclusion

1. The Quantum Imperative for Leadership

As we stand at the precipice of a new era, **the quantum age of business**, the urgency for transformation has never been greater. The **rules of wealth, leadership, and value creation are being rewritten** by forces that can no longer be ignored—**Artificial Intelligence (AI) and Sustainability**. These twin forces, far from being independent, are deeply entangled in shaping the next phase of conscious capitalism and organizational decision-making.

Traditional leadership frameworks are rapidly becoming obsolete. The relentless pace of AI-driven automation is dismantling industries overnight, while the accelerating climate crisis is forcing businesses to confront their role in either **perpetuating destruction or pioneering regeneration**. C-suite leaders **must act now**—not in a few years, not when their industries are forced to comply, but immediately, with **decisive and conscious action**.

The New Leadership Paradigm: Conscious Decision-Making in an AI-Driven World

Leadership in the quantum era demands an **expansive, multi-dimensional approach**—one that fuses **data-driven intelligence with ethical consciousness**, balancing **technological acceleration**

with sustainability. Conscious decision-making is no longer an option; it is the defining characteristic of the leaders who will thrive.

1. **AI as a Tool for Regenerative Capitalism:** Leaders must move beyond seeing AI as merely an efficiency booster. AI should be leveraged to **solve systemic global challenges**, from optimizing resource use to predicting and mitigating climate risks in supply chains. AI can analyze vast amounts of data at speeds beyond human capability, identifying patterns and solutions that can drive **carbon neutrality, circular economy transitions, and ethical supply chain management**. The conscious leader must not only adopt AI but also ensure that it serves **humanity and the planet** rather than reinforcing existing inequalities.

2. **Ethical AI Deployment:** The speed at which AI is evolving requires leaders to be vigilant in ensuring its **responsible and conscious application**. This means establishing **AI governance frameworks** that prioritize transparency, fairness, and human-centric outcomes. AI systems must be **auditable, explainable, and aligned with corporate values** to prevent unethical biases or exploitation. Furthermore, leaders must ensure that AI-driven decisions align with **long-term planetary sustainability and social responsibility**.

3. **Conscious Decision-Making Over Profit Maximization:** The short-term, quarterly-profit mindset must evolve into **long-term, planetary stewardship**. Organizations that operate with **a triple-bottom-line approach—people, planet, and profit—will outlast those who chase short-term gains at the expense of sustainability.** Leaders must set **impact-driven KPIs** that evaluate **social equity, ecological footprint, and technological ethics** alongside financial performance, ensuring that business success is measured holistically.

Conscious Capitalism: The New Wealth Model

Quantum wealth is not about **hoarding financial capital** but about **expanding holistic value—social, ecological, and intellectual capital**. The age of **exploitative capitalism is over**; conscious capitalism, fueled by AI and sustainability, is the new standard.

1. **Businesses as Stewards of the Future:** Companies must **redefine success** as more than just shareholder returns. The highest-performing businesses of the next decade will be those that embed **circular economy models, carbon neutrality, and regenerative business practices** into their core strategies. Leaders must build companies that function as **ecosystem contributors**, ensuring that wealth creation **enhances rather than extracts** from the world.
2. **Collaboration Over Competition:** Quantum wealth creation is **network-driven**. Leaders must **actively forge alliances across industries** to co-create solutions that transcend zero-sum thinking. Businesses must participate in **public-private partnerships, open innovation networks, and cooperative AI models** that drive systemic change beyond individual corporate interests.
3. **Redefining Leadership Compensation:** Executive rewards must be tied to long-term sustainability metrics rather than short-term stock price gains. Leaders must be accountable for the planetary and social impact of their decisions. Compensation structures should incentivize **sustainability outcomes, ethical AI deployment, and human capital development**, ensuring that leadership performance is measured by **legacy, not just profit.**

The Quantum Action Plan: Steps to Begin Now

To catalyze this transformation, leaders must take immediate, strategic action. Below is a **concrete plan** to begin the shift toward

Quantum Wealth Creation, Conscious Capitalism, and AI-Driven Sustainability.

Step 1: Conduct a Quantum Business Audit

- Evaluate your organization's **alignment with AI and sustainability**—where are the gaps?
- Identify areas where **AI can drive conscious, sustainable innovations**, from operations to customer engagement.
- Assess **your leadership team's awareness and preparedness** for ethical AI deployment and sustainability-driven business models.

Step 2: Integrate AI-Driven Sustainability Metrics

- Establish **real-time AI-powered sustainability tracking systems** to monitor carbon footprints, resource use, and social impact.
- Implement **climate-conscious financial modeling**, considering **long-term ecological risks and opportunities**.
- Begin **data-driven impact measurement**, ensuring every strategic move aligns with regenerative capitalism.

Step 3: Cultivate a Culture of Conscious Decision-Making

- Train leadership teams in **quantum decision frameworks** that incorporate AI insights and **sustainability imperatives**.
- Shift organizational KPIs from **profit-first to impact-first**, aligning business success with long-term ecological and social well-being.
- Implement AI-assisted ethical governance frameworks that **evaluate the long-term societal impact of business decisions.**

Step 4: Transition to Quantum Wealth Networks

- Form **cross-industry alliances** to **share AI and sustainability innovations**, ensuring collective progress.
- Invest in **regenerative ecosystems**—not just individual sustainability initiatives, but **large-scale, industry-wide collaborations.**
- Partner with AI developers committed to **ethical, sustainable advancements** to co-create AI models that enhance human and environmental prosperity.

Step 5: Set a 5-Year Vision for Quantum Prosperity

- Define **your organization's quantum leadership blueprint**, outlining **AI integration, sustainability commitments, and conscious capitalism milestones**.
- Reframe **your investment strategies** to align with **long-term planetary regeneration and social impact**.
- Publicly commit to **a Quantum Conscious Capitalism roadmap**, setting transparent goals and accountability mechanisms that ensure real transformation.

The Future Belongs to the Quantum Leader

The next decade will belong to those who have the **courage to think beyond traditional paradigms**, who **embrace the unknown with curiosity**, and who take **decisive action toward building a world where AI serves humanity and wealth is regenerative.**

The cost of inaction is extinction—**not just for businesses, but for the very systems that sustain life on Earth**. As a C-suite leader, your legacy will be defined by the **choices you make today. Will you choose stagnation or transformation? Will you lead with consciousness or be led by outdated systems?**

This is your moment to step into **quantum leadership**, to become a **catalyst for change, a steward of wealth, and a pioneer of a new era in business.** The blueprint is here. The action is yours to take.

The time to act is now.

Reflection

Acknowledgments

This book would not exist without the contributions of many individuals. My deepest gratitude goes to my mentors, whose wisdom and guidance have shaped my understanding of conscious business and leadership. Their unwavering support and belief in my vision have been invaluable. I am also profoundly thankful to the numerous conscious business leaders and entrepreneurs I've had the privilege of working with and learning from. Their stories, experiences, and insights have enriched this work immeasurably. A special thanks to [Name(s) of specific individuals], whose contributions were particularly impactful.

My sincere appreciation also extends to [Publisher's Name] and the editorial team, whose expertise and dedication transformed the manuscript into the finished product. Their commitment to quality and attention to detail was exceptional. Finally, I thank my family and friends for their unwavering patience and support throughout the writing process. Their love and encouragement provided the strength and inspiration I needed to complete this project.

Glossary

Conscious Business:
A business model that prioritizes purpose, people, planet, and profit, operating with ethical consciousness and social responsibility.

Regenerative Practices:
Business strategies that actively restore and enhance the natural environment, exceeding mere sustainability.

Holistic Leadership:
Leadership that integrates personal growth, ethical awareness, and social responsibility, fostering a culture of collaboration, trust, and empowerment.

Stakeholder Capitalism:
An economic system that prioritizes the needs and well-being of all stakeholders –employees, customers, suppliers, communities, and the environment – not just shareholders.

Emotional Intelligence:
The ability to understand and manage one's own emotions and the emotions of others, leading to effective communication, collaboration, and conflict resolution.

Mindfulness:

A state of present moment awareness cultivated through practices such as meditation, enabling greater self-awareness, focus, and compassion.

References

Banker, D. V., & Bhal, K. T. (2018). Understanding Compassion from Practicing Managers' Perspective: Vicious and Virtuous Forces in Business Organizations. *Global Business Review, 21*(1), 262-278. https://doi.org/10.1177/0972150917749279 (Original work published 2020)

Barnosky, D., Matzke, N., Tomiya, S., Wogan, G. O. U., Swartz, B., Quental, T. B., Marshall, C., McGuire, J. L., Lindsey, E. L., Maguire, K. C., Mersey, B., & Ferrer, E. A. 2011. Has the Earth's sixth mass extinction already arrived? **Nature**, 471: 51–57. Google Scholar

Clement, V., Rigaud, K. K., de Sherbinin, A., Jones, B., Adamo, S., Schewe, J., Sadiq, N., & Shabahat, E. 2021. Groundswell part 2: Acting on internal climate migration. Retrieved from https://openknowledge.worldbank.org/entities/publication/2c9150df-52c3-58ed-9075-d78ea56c3267 Google Scholar

Della Valle, E., Palermi, S., Aloe, I., Marcantonio, R., Spera, R., Montagnani, S., & Sirico, F. (2020). Effectiveness of Workplace Yoga Interventions to Reduce Perceived Stress in Employees: A Systematic Review and Meta-Analysis. *Journal of functional morphology and kinesiology, 5*(2), 33. https://doi.org/10.3390/jfmk5020033

Financial Times, 2019. FT Sets the Agenda With a New Brand Platform. 16 September 2019. https://aboutus.ft.com/press_release/ft-sets-the-agenda-with-new-brand-platform.

Flavelle, C. 2021. April 22: Climate change could cut world economy by $23 trillion in 2050, insurance giant warns. New York Times. Google Scholar

Heron, K. (2024). Capitalist catastrophism and eco-apartheid. *Geoforum*, *153*, 103874. https://doi.org/10.1016/j.geoforum.2023.103874

Tooze, A. (2021). *Shutdown: How Covid shook the world's economy*. Penguin UK.

Tooze, A. (2023). Welcome to the World of the Polycrisis. The Financial Times. 28 October 2023. https://www.ft.com/content/498398e7-11b1-494b-9cd3-6d669dc3de33

UNFCCC. 2023. COP28 agreement signals "beginning of the end" of the fossil fuel era. Retrieved from https://unfccc.int/news/cop28-agreement-signals-beginning-of-the-end-of-the-fossil-fuel-eraGoogle Scholar

Author Biography

Jivi Saran, MBA, DBA(c) is a professor of business, executive coach, and founder of *Quantum Business*, a global movement committed to reimagining the future of leadership. With an MBA from Royal Roads University and a Doctorate in Business Administration in progress, she brings a rare blend of academic depth, strategic insight, and human-centered wisdom to her work with organizations and leaders around the world.

Drawing on over two decades of experience in leadership development, executive coaching, and systems transformation, Jivi's approach is grounded in the belief that **business is not only a driver of economic progress—it is a catalyst for human and planetary wellbeing.** Her lifelong inquiry into **consciousness, self-excellence**, and collective intelligence has shaped a powerful question: *How can we lead with humble hearts and high intellect in a rapidly evolving world?*

Her answer is *Quantum Business*—a framework that empowers leaders to integrate spiritual intelligence, ethical decision-making, and systems thinking into the core of enterprise. In her work, business becomes more than a machine—it becomes a living system, designed to serve people, planet, and purpose.

Jivi's vision for the future of business is clear: **organizations must become regenerative, deeply human, and prepared not just to survive disruption, but to lead meaningful transformation.** Her latest book offers a roadmap to this future—where leadership begins with self-awareness, and success is measured not just by scale, but by significance.

Jivi Saran, MBA, DBA(c)

At this pivotal moment in history, Jivi invites leaders to rise—not in isolation, but in unity. With humility, clarity, and a fierce sense of responsibility, she calls us to build what the world needs most: conscious enterprises led by conscious humans.

Manufactured by Amazon.ca
Acheson, AB